最新時事テーマ収録
Readings for ADVANCED English Learners

Cutting Edge

ナビブック 付

速読トレーニング
文構造解説
重要語句

難関大対応

Orange

本書は、入試完成レベルの英文読解力を段階的に養成できるように編集されています。

英文素材について

① 新しい素材で、「読む価値がある英文」であること
② 文系・理系のテーマのバランスを取ること
③ 難易度にバラつきがでないこと
を基準に厳選しました。そうして選ばれた英文を、段階的に難関大入試レベルの読解力を養成できるように配列しています。

設問について

「構文・語彙」など入試の設問になりやすい部分と、内容理解のポイントとなる部分に、英文の流れに沿って設問を配置しています。設問をはじめから解いていくことで、内容が理解できる構成になっています。

「Navi Book」について

英文学習をより深く、より効率的なものにするためにも付属「Navi Book」の活用をおすすめいたします。「Navi Book」では、英文内の重要語句がレベル別にほぼ全て網羅されています。また「英単語」→「日本語の意味」の順で読み上げた音声と一緒に確認することで、より効果的な学習ができるようになっています。英文中の分かりづらい構文や複雑な文構造についても解説していますので、わからなかった英文については問題を解いた後にしっかりと確認しましょう。加えて、国公立大学二次試験に必須の「要約力」、「記述力」を養える要約問題も用意しています。

背景情報について

英文を読む上で、その英文の中で扱われている内容についての知識があることは大きな武器になります。本書では「テーマ解説」を用意しています。テーマの背景情報だけでなく、ウラ話、さらに入試情報なども織り交ぜた、読み応えのある内容になっています。

【本書の設問について】

設問指示文右端の大学名は、出題校で実際に出題された問題、改は一部改題の問題です。その他の設問は、出題傾向、難易度、記述・客観のバランスに合わせて作成されたオリジナル問題です。

Chapter 1

The recipe for making any creature is written in its DNA. So last year, when geneticists* published the near-complete DNA sequence of the long-extinct woolly mammoth, there was much speculation about whether we could bring this giant creature back to life.

5　Creating a living, breathing creature from a genome* sequence that exists only in a computer's memory is not possible right now. But someone someday is sure to try it, predicts Stephan Schuster, a molecular biologist at Pennsylvania State University and a driving force behind the mammoth genome project.

So besides the mammoth, what other extinct beasts might we bring back to life? Well, 10　it is only going to be possible with creatures for which we can recover a complete genome sequence. (1)Without one, there is no chance. And usually when a creature dies, the DNA in any flesh left untouched is soon destroyed as it is attacked by sunshine and bacteria.

There are, however, some circumstances in which DNA can be preserved. If your 15　specimen froze to death in an icy wasteland such as Siberia, or died in a dark cave or a really dry region, for instance, then the probability of finding some intact stretches of DNA is much higher.

Even in ideal conditions, though, no genetic information is likely to survive more than a million years — so dinosaurs are out — and only much younger remains are likely 20　to yield good-quality DNA. "It's really only worth studying specimens that are less than 100,000 years old," says Schuster.

The genomes of several extinct species besides the mammoth are already being sequenced, but (2)turning these into living creatures will not be easy. "It's hard to say that something will never ever be possible," says Svante Pääbo of the Max Planck Institute 25　for Evolutionary Anthropology in Germany, "but it would require technologies so far removed from what we currently have that I cannot imagine how it would be done."

But then (3)50 years ago, who would have believed we would now be able to read the instructions for making humans, fix inherited diseases, clone mammals and be close to creating artificial life? Assuming that we will develop the necessary technology, we have 30　selected ten extinct creatures that might one day be resurrected. Our choice is based not just on practicality, but also on each animal's "charisma" — just how exciting the prospect of resurrecting these animals is.

Of course, bringing extinct creatures back to life raises a number of further problems, such as where they will live, but let's not (4).

* geneticist「遺伝学者」 genome「ゲノム (生物の生活機能を維持するための最小限の遺伝子群を含む染色体の一組)」

1 下線部 (1) を書き換えるとき、空所 (A) (B) それぞれに入る数語を答えなさい。 (東京理科大・改)

Without (A)(   ), there is no chance of
(B)(   ).

2 死滅した動物の DNA 抽出の可能性が高くなる条件 2 つを、本文の内容に即して日本語で説明しなさい。

・ ....

・ ....

3 下線部 (2) に関し、これが容易でないのはなぜか、日本語で説明しなさい。

....

4 下線部 (3) を日本語に直しなさい。 (東京理科大・改)

....

....

....

5 今後の技術の進歩を想定して筆者たちは現在どんな試みをしているか、But then ... から始まる第 7 段落の内容に即して日本語で説明しなさい。

....

6 空所 (4) に入れるのに最も適切なものを 1 つ選びなさい。 (東京理科大)

① admit the mistakes ② deny evolution ③ ignore scientists ④ spoil the fun

7 本文の内容と一致しないものを 1 つ選びなさい。 (東京理科大)

① When scientists published the near-complete DNA sequence of the mammoth, many people wondered if it would be possible to have a living mammoth once again on this planet.

② Stephan Schuster is playing a major role in recovering the genome sequence of the mammoth.

③ Stephan Schuster says that he will be able to create a mammoth himself when all of its genome sequence has been recovered.

④ The mammoth is not the only extinct species whose genome sequence has been studied.

⑤ The author is aware that there are problems other than just the technological ones to be solved in order to resurrect extinct species.

Chapter 2

There is a dirty little secret known to health professionals that they do not usually ⊙1-9 much talk about. Let's assume that you follow the recommendations of a health authority and get out there most days to go jogging, even though you would much rather be doing something else. Say you get ready, warm up, jog, and cool down for
5 about an hour a day, which is a modest regimen.

Over a year, you will spend about 360 hours doing this, and during 40 years (say, ⊙1-10 from age twenty-one to age sixty-one), you will spend about (X) hours. Assuming that most of us are awake for about 16 hours a day, this means that you would be spending the equivalent of about (Y) days jogging. This is about two and a half
10 years spent exercising.

How much longer would such an active person live? How many extra days of life ⊙1-11 would this diligent jogger gain in which to pursue other well-loved hobbies? We do not know for sure, but anything that increased average (Z) by more than two and a half years in a generally healthy adult population would be considered a very large effect
15 — a striking phenomenon. (1)So, with two and a half years spent on the pavement, there is not likely to be much of a net* gain in available time for our poor jogger. Anyone who exercised even more would gain even less, winding up with a net loss of time. But it gets even worse. Note that in this contrived example, the unhappy jogger is trading away thousands of hours of youth for perhaps a few extra years in old age.
20 Many individuals would not choose (2)that trade-off. They would prefer to have their leisure time when they are young and healthy.

Of course the real picture is somewhat more complicated. The jogger might really ⊙1-12 enjoy jogging and so might consider the time well spent. Or the jogger might be warding off a diagnosed tendency toward a debilitating chronic disease such as diabetes.
25 (3)Still, for many reasonably healthy and active individuals who are out running every morning because some advice list or some friend is pressuring them to try to improve their health, the results are not necessarily going to be what they expect. Some might have better uses for all that time, and others will be harmed by running injuries or even sudden death from cardiac arrest.

30 From a public health point of view, it's great that so many people these days like ⊙1-13 to engage in socially hyped challenges like marathons. (4)But it is important to recognize that these are recent social phenomena, and that many people in the past remained

steadily active in a healthy way having never even heard of a jogging trail or a spinning class★.

1 空所 (X) (Y) に入る数字を書きなさい。 　　　　　　　　　　　　　　　　　　　　(兵庫医科大)

(X)..　　　　　(Y)..

2 空所 (Z) に入る最も適切な 1 語を選びなさい。

①　intelligence　　②　loss　　③　productivity　　④　longevity　　⑤　output

3　下線部 (1) で述べられている、ジョギングする時間と人生の時間の関連について、80 字以内（句読点を含む）の日本語でまとめなさい。

									10										20

4　下線部 (2) の内容を日本語で説明しなさい。 　　　　　　　　　　　　　　　　　　(兵庫医科大・改)

5　下線部 (3) を日本語に直しなさい。

6　下線部 (4) を日本語に直しなさい。

7　本文の内容と一致するものを 1 つ選びなさい。

①　Health professionals are not supposed to advise people to go out jogging, because it is a dirty secret.

②　Active young people are aware that they should pursue their favorite hobbies instead of spending many hours jogging.

③　Jogging is not always going to give the people engaged in it the results that they expect of it.

④　Public health professionals recommend marathon rather than jogging because marathon is a more social challenge.

⑤　Compared to people today, the people in the past were less healthy because of their inactive participation in jogging.

Chapter 3

This actually did happen to a real person, and the real person is me. I had gone to ⊙1-18 catch a train. This was April 1976, in Cambridge, U.K. I was a bit early for the train. I'd gotten the time of the train wrong. I went to get myself a newspaper to do the crossword, and a cup of coffee and a packet of cookies. I went and sat at a table. I want

5 you to picture the scene. It's very important that you get this very clear in your mind. Here's the table, newspaper, cup of coffee, packet of cookies. There's a guy sitting opposite me, perfectly ordinary-looking guy wearing a business suit, carrying a briefcase. It didn't look like he was going to do anything weird. What he did was this: he suddenly leaned across, picked up the packet of cookies, tore it open, took one out, and ate it.

10 Now (1)this, I have to say, is the sort of thing the British are very bad at dealing with. ⊙1-19 There's nothing in our background, upbringing, or education that teaches you how to deal with someone who in broad daylight has just stolen your cookies. You know what would happen if this had been South Central Los Angeles. There would have very quickly been gunfire, helicopters coming in, CNN, you know ... But in the end, I did

15 what any red-blooded Englishman would do: [2]. And I stared at the newspaper, took a sip of coffee, tried to do a clue in the newspaper, couldn't do anything, and thought, *What am I going to do?*

In the end I thought, *Nothing for it, I'll just have to go for it*, and I tried very hard not ⊙1-20 to notice the fact that the packet was already mysteriously opened. I took out a cookie

20 for myself. I thought, *That settled him.* But (3)it hadn't because a moment or two later he did it again. He took another cookie. Having not mentioned it the first time, it was somehow even harder to raise the subject the second time around. "Excuse me, I couldn't help but (4)notice ..." I mean, it doesn't really work.

We went through the whole packet like this. When I say the whole packet, I mean ⊙1-21

25 there were only about eight cookies, but it felt like a lifetime. He took one, I took one, he took one, I took one. Finally, when we got to the end, he stood up and walked away. Well, we exchanged meaningful looks, then he walked away, and I breathed a sigh of relief and sat back.

A moment or two later the train was coming in, so I tossed back the rest of my ⊙1-22

30 coffee, stood up, picked up the newspaper, and underneath the newspaper were my cookies. The thing I like particularly about this story is the sensation that somewhere in England there has been wandering around for the last quarter-century a perfectly

ordinary guy who's had the same exact story, only he doesn't have (5)the punch line.

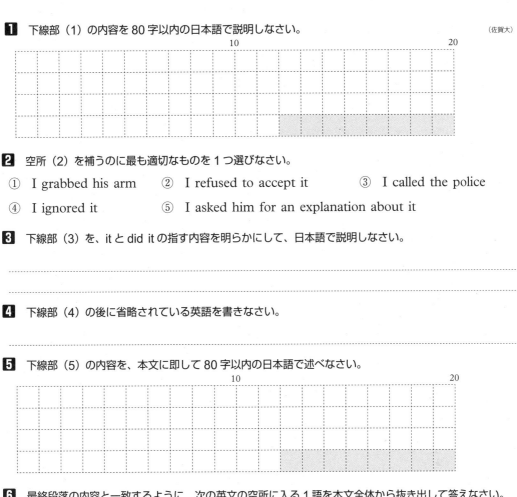

1 下線部（1）の内容を 80 字以内の日本語で説明しなさい。 (佐賀大)

2 空所（2）を補うのに最も適切なものを 1 つ選びなさい。

① I grabbed his arm　　② I refused to accept it　　③ I called the police

④ I ignored it　　⑤ I asked him for an explanation about it

3 下線部（3）を、it と did it の指す内容を明らかにして、日本語で説明しなさい。

4 下線部（4）の後に省略されている英語を書きなさい。

5 下線部（5）の内容を、本文に即して 80 字以内の日本語で述べなさい。

6 最終段落の内容と一致するように、次の英文の空所に入る 1 語を本文全体から抜き出して答えなさい。

If the writer hadn't picked up the newspaper, he would have walked around for the rest of his life believing that the other guy was pretty (　　　　　).

7 本文の内容と一致しないものを 2 つ選びなさい。

① The writer arrived at the station a little early because his watch didn't keep correct time.

② When the writer saw the man in a business suit sitting opposite him, he didn't think that the guy would steal his cookies.

③ Seeing one of his cookies eaten by the total stranger, the writer behaved calmly just as his upbringing and education had taught him to.

④ The guy and the writer kept eating cookies alternately until the whole packet was empty.

⑤ Not until the train came and the writer picked up the newspaper did he find that he was the one who was "the weird guy."

Chapter 4

The English language is full of words which have changed their meanings slightly 🔊1-27 or even dramatically over the centuries. Changes of meaning can be of a number of different types. Some words, such as *nice*, have changed gradually. Emotive words tend to change more rapidly by losing some of their force, so that *awful*, which originally
5 meant 'inspiring awe', now means 'very bad' or, in expressions such as *awfully good*, simply something like 'very'. In any case, all connection with 'awe' has been lost.

Some changes of meaning, though, seem to attract more attention than others. 🔊1-28 (1)This is perhaps particularly the case where the people who worry about such things believe that a distinction is being lost. For example, there is a lot of concern at the
10 moment about the words *uninterested* and *disinterested*. In modern English, the positive form *interested* has two different meanings. The first and older meaning is approximately 'having a personal involvement in', as in

　　He is an interested party in the dispute.

The second and later, but now much more common, meaning is 'demonstrating or
15 experiencing curiosity in, enthusiasm for, concern for,' as in

　　He is very interested in cricket.

(2)It is not a problem that this word has more than one meaning. Confusion never seems to occur, largely because the context will normally make it obvious which meaning is intended. In all human languages there are very many words which have more than
20 one meaning — this is a very common and entirely normal (3)state of affairs. Most English speakers, for example, can instantly think of a number of different meanings for the words *common* and *state* and *affairs* which I have just used.

Perhaps surprisingly, according to dictionaries the two different meanings of *interested* 🔊1-29 have different negative forms. The negative of the first meaning is *disinterested*, as in

25 (4)*He is an interested party in the dispute, and I am disinterested and therefore able to be more objective about it.*

Disinterested is thus roughly equivalent to 'neutral, impartial'. The negative form of the second, more usual meaning is *uninterested*, as in

　　He is very interested in cricket, but I am uninterested in all sports.

30 *Uninterested* is thus roughly equivalent to 'bored, feeling no curiosity'.

Now it happens that *interested*, in its original meaning, is today a rather unusual, learned, formal word in English. Most people, if they wanted to convey this concept in normal everyday speech, would probably say something like *not neutral*, or *biased* or *involved* or *concerned*. Recently, this unfamiliarity with the older meaning of the word (A) has led to many people now using (B) with the same meaning as (C):   35

I am disinterested in cricket.

They have, perhaps, heard the word (D) and, not being aware of the meaning 'neutral, unbiased', they have started using it as the negative form of (E) in the more recent sense. Opponents of this change claim that this is an ignorant misuse of the word, and that a very useful distinction is being lost. What can we say about this?   40

1 下線部（1）を、This の指す内容を明らかにしながら日本語に直しなさい。　　　　　　(神戸大・改)

....
....
....

2 下線部（2）に関し、なぜこのように言えるのか、本文に即して日本語で説明しなさい。

....
....

3 下線部（3）のこの文脈における意味と同じ意味で使われているものを 1 つ選びなさい。

① A **state** occasion is a formal one involving the head of a country.
② When you talk about the **state** of someone or something, you are referring to the condition they are in or what they are like at a particular time.
③ If you **state** something, you say or write it in a formal or definite way.
④ If the dead body of an important person lies in **state**, it is publicly displayed for a few days before it is buried.

4 下線部（4）を日本語に直しなさい。

....
....

5 Fill in the blanks (A) to (E) with the most suitable word below. Write the numbers ① to ③ that correspond to your answer. Each word can be used more than once.   (神戸大)

① interested   ② uninterested   ③ disinterested

(A)................   (B)................   (C)................   (D)................   (E)................

次ページへ続く→

6 Which of the following statements match the content of the text?　Select two most suitable statements from ① to ⑤.　(神戸大)

① It is not appropriate to use the phrase "awfully good" when you praise someone for his/her achievement because it is too emotional an expression.

② Some people say "I am disinterested in cricket", meaning they are not interested in cricket.

③ The word "uninterested" has two meanings because words with two meanings are a common and normal state of affairs.

④ When you are having a personal involvement in a dispute, you are not a disinterested party in it.

⑤ According to the text, it is safe to say that the distinction between the two negative forms of *interested* has been totally lost today.

Chapter 5

1-35 When Mike May was three years old, a chemical explosion rendered him completely blind. This did not stop him from becoming the best blind downhill speed skier in the world, as well as a businessman and family man. Then, forty-three years after the explosion robbed him of his vision, he heard about a new surgical development that might be able to restore it. Although he was successful in his life as a blind man, he decided to undergo the surgery.

1-36 After the operation, the bandages were removed from around his eyes. Accompanied by a photographer, Mike sat on a chair while his two children were brought in. This was a big moment. It would be the first time he would ever gaze into their faces with his newly cleared eyes. In the resulting photograph, Mike has a pleasant but awkward smile on his face as his children smile at him.

1-37 (1)The scene was supposed to be touching, but it wasn't. There was a problem. Mike's eyes were now working perfectly, but he stared with utter puzzlement at the objects in front of him. His brain didn't know what to make of the overwhelming flow of information. He wasn't experiencing his sons' faces; he was experiencing only uninterpretable sensations of edges and colors and lights. Although his eyes were functioning, he didn't have vision.

1-38 And this is because the brain has to learn how to see. The strange electrical storms inside the pitch-black skull get turned into conscious summaries after a sustained effort of figuring out how objects in the world match up across the senses. Consider the experience of walking down a hallway. Mike knew from a lifetime of moving down corridors that walls remain parallel, at arm's length, the whole way down. So when his vision was restored, the concept of perspective lines meeting at a distant point was beyond his capacity to understand. (2)It made no sense to his brain.

1-39 Similarly, when I was a child I met a blind woman and was amazed at how intimately she knew the layout of her rooms and furniture. I asked her if she would be able to draw the layouts with higher accuracy than most sighted people. Her response surprised me: she said she would not be able to draw the layouts at all, because she didn't understand how sighted people converted three dimensions (the room) into two dimensions (a flat piece of paper). (3)The idea simply didn't make sense to her.

1-40 Vision does not simply exist when a person confronts the world with clear eyes. Instead, an interpretation of the electro-chemical signals streaming from the eyes to the

brain has to be trained up. Mike's brain didn't understand how his own movements affected the way he saw objects. For example, when he moves his head to the left, the
35 scene shifts to the right. The brains of sighted people have come to expect such things and know how to ignore them. But Mike's brain was confused by these strange relationships. And this illustrates a key point: the conscious experience of vision occurs only when there is accurate prediction of sensory consequences. (4)So although vision seems like a representation of something that's objectively out there, it doesn't come for
40 free. It has to be learned.

After moving around for several weeks, staring at things, kicking chairs, examining ◉1-41 silverware, rubbing his wife's face, Mike came to have the experience of sight as we experience it. He now experiences vision the same way you do. He just appreciates it more.

1 下線部（1）に関し、以下の質問に答えなさい。
（ア）The scene とはどんな場面か、日本語で説明しなさい。

....
....

（イ）it wasn't と述べられている理由を日本語で説明しなさい。

....
....
....

2 下線部（2）に関し、以下の質問に答えなさい。
（ア）下線部を、It の指すものを明らかにしながら日本語に直しなさい。

....
....

（イ）下線部について、その理由を日本語で説明しなさい。

....
....

3 下線部（3）の内容を日本語で説明しなさい。 （千葉大）

....

4 下線部（4）をわかりやすい日本語に直しなさい。

----

5 本文の内容と一致するものを 2 つ選びなさい。

① Mike decided to undergo the eye surgery because he wanted to achieve success in another field.

② When Mike first saw his children's smiling faces after the operation, he was so moved by the scene that he couldn't believe his eyes.

③ Though Mike's eyes were functioning perfectly after the surgery, his brain had to learn how to see.

④ The writer was amazed to find that the blind woman could draw accurately two-dimensional layouts of her rooms and furniture on a piece of paper.

⑤ Mike made a sustained effort for several weeks before he came to experience sight as sighted people do.

Chapter 6

Climate change isn't new. Our planet is always changing and its environment ⊚ 1-46
rarely stays still for long. There have been times in the distant past when levels of
CO_2 were much higher than they are today, and Antarctica, a continent around the
South Pole, was a tropical paradise. There have been others when CO_2 levels were
5 much lower, and there was even ice in what are now tropical areas. But over the past
ten thousand years the Earth's climate has been unusually steady. We humans have
become used to a world where the temperature hasn't changed much. In other words,
we have been lucky. Now our steady reliable climate is changing, and this time nature
isn't to blame. But how do we know for certain that the world is warming?

10 When you're trying to determine whether the world's temperature is rising, the ⊚ 1-47
biggest problem is picking out a signal from the "background noise." Even in our
relatively stable times, temperatures move up and down from one day to another,
from season to season, from year to year, and from place to place. To be sure that
(1)the trend is occurring, you need to take precise measurements from many different
15 places around the world, and do so for an extremely long time. The world's longest
survey is (2)the Central England Temperature Record, which is a result of the serious
data-collecting habits of seventeenth-century British natural scientists. It covers a
large region of England and stretches back to 1659. The impressive record shows
clear signs of warming, especially toward the end of the twentieth century.

20 However, the record covers only a tiny part of the globe. Changes in England ⊚ 1-48
don't necessarily reflect changes in the United States or Brazil. It also doesn't go
back far enough to reveal just how unusual our recent warm temperatures really are.
How do they compare, for instance, to the apparent warm period in medieval times
when grapes were grown in northern England? Or to the so-called Little Ice Age
25 several hundred years ago, when the River Thames in London froze over completely
so that people could gather and sell things on its solid surface? To answer these
questions, scientists have come up with clever ways to expand the records
geographically and extend them backward in time. These records are written not by
humans, but by nature.

30 Every year, the average tree grows a ring of new wood around its trunk. In a ⊚ 1-49
good year the ring will be thicker, in a bad year, thinner. Researchers drill a small
core into the side of the tree, about the size of a wine cork, take out the wood, and
then count and measure. By examining trees that are different ages, (3)they have been

able to create a temperature record extending more than a thousand years and from regions across northern Europe, Russia, and North America. 35

1-50   In the frozen north and south, ice also contains a record book of past climate. Each year's snowfall buries the previous one. If temperatures are cold enough, the snow stays around long enough to be squeezed into ice, clearly marking out the annual layers because summer's snow crystals are larger than winter's, or because more dust blows in each year with the winter winds. (4)The amount of snow that fell 40 in a given year gives clues as to how warm it was then.

1-51   By fitting together a variety of measures like these, researchers have come to remarkably similar conclusions about temperatures over the last thousand years. The eleventh century was indeed relatively warm, corresponding to the Medieval Warm Period. Temperatures were cooler in the seventeenth century, corresponding to the 45 Little Ice Age, and again in the early nineteenth century. These warm and cool periods apparently were also fairly widespread.

1-52   However, it was only in the twentieth century that temperatures really began to rise noticeably. The warming didn't happen regularly, but in two bursts — which turns out to be important. The first one occurred during the early years of the 50 century and was marked enough that it made itself clearly felt. The second burst of warming began in the 1970s and has been gathering pace ever since. And, crucially, the temperatures we are experiencing now are hotter than they have been for the entire last thousand years. Even the Medieval Warm Period was cooler than it is today. 55

1-53   Let's look at some numbers. On a global scale, from the 1910s to the 1940s, average temperatures rose by about 0.3°C. After that there was a cooling of about 0.1°C, and since 1970 the world has warmed by a further 0.6°C. These numbers might not sound like much, but they are very significant. (5)Although the temperature where you live can change by much more than this within the space of a few hours 60 or days, it is much more worrying when global annual averages show a clear upward trend. Averaging in this way smooths out short-term differences and shows what's really happening. That's why a small change in global average temperature can reflect a very big shift in climate. Speaking in global averages, only a few degrees separate us from the frozen world of the last ice age. 65

1 本文の内容に照らして、空所に入る最も適当なものを 1 つ選びなさい。   (関西大)

The first paragraph suggests that over the last ten thousand years _____.
① icy and tropical conditions lasted for long periods of time
② CO_2 levels have been much higher than they are today
③ the climate of the Earth has changed relatively little

次ページへ続く→

2 下線部（1）が指す内容は何か、第2段落中から英語をそのまま抜き出して答えなさい。

....

3 下線部（2）に関し、そのデータとしての欠点として指摘されている2点を、本文の内容に即して日本語で簡潔に述べなさい。

・
....
....
・
....
....

4 下線部（3）が指すものは何か、本文中から英語を抜き出して答えなさい。 （関西大・改）

....

5 下線部（4）を日本語に直しなさい。

....
....

6 本文の内容に照らして、空所に入る最も適当なものを1つ選びなさい。 （関西大）

According to the sixth and the seventh paragraphs, _____.

① many researchers believe that the Medieval Warm Period was actually cooler than previously thought

② in the eleventh and seventeenth centuries temperature changes were similar in scale to those of the twentieth century

③ temperature changes in the twentieth century were more extreme than those experienced in earlier centuries

7 下線部（5）を日本語に直しなさい。

....
....
....

8 本文の内容と一致しないものを1つ選びなさい。 （関西大・改）

① Global warming is hard to measure because temperatures tend to change often even during otherwise steady times.

② The Central England Temperature Record shows a warming trend toward the end of the twentieth century.

③ Different phenomena of nature like annual rings of trees and ice layers provide information about temperatures in the past.

④ Minor variations in temperature have little effect on global warming.

Memo

(1)<u>We are, to a remarkable degree, the right distance from the right sort of star,</u> one ⏏1-58 that is big enough to radiate lots of energy, but not so big as to burn itself out swiftly. It is a curiosity of physics that the larger a star the more rapidly it burns. Had our sun been ten times as massive, it would have exhausted itself after ten million years instead of ten billion and we wouldn't be here now. We are also fortunate to orbit where we do. Too much nearer and everything on Earth would have boiled away. Much farther away and everything would have frozen.

In 1978, an astrophysicist named Michael Hart made some calculations and ⏏1-59 concluded that Earth would have been uninhabitable had it been just 1 percent farther from or 5 percent closer to the Sun. (2)<u>That's not much, and in fact it wasn't enough.</u> The figures have since been refined and made a little more generous — 5 percent nearer and 15 percent farther are thought to be more accurate assessments for our zone of habitability — but that is still a narrow belt.

To appreciate just how narrow, you have only to look at Venus. Venus is only ⏏1-60 twenty-five million miles closer to the Sun than we are. The Sun's warmth reaches it just two minutes before it touches us. In size and composition, Venus is very like Earth, but the small difference in orbital distance made all the difference to (3)<u>how it turned out.</u> It appears that during the early years of the solar system Venus was only slightly warmer than Earth and probably had oceans. But those few degrees of extra warmth meant that Venus could not hold on to its surface water, with disastrous consequences for its climate. As its water evaporated, the hydrogen atoms escaped into space, and the oxygen atoms combined with carbon to form a dense atmosphere of the greenhouse gas CO_2. Venus became stifling. Although people of my age will recall a time when astronomers hoped that Venus might harbor life beneath its padded clouds, possibly even a kind of tropical vegetation, we now know that it is much too fierce an environment for any kind of life that we can reasonably conceive of. Its surface temperature is a roasting 470 degrees centigrade (roughly 900 degrees Fahrenheit), which is hot enough to melt lead, and the atmospheric pressure at the surface is ninety times that of Earth, or more than any human body could withstand. We lack the technology to make suits or even spaceships that would allow us to visit. Our knowledge of Venus's surface is based on distant radar imagery and some disturbing noise from an unmanned Soviet probe that was dropped hopefully into the clouds in 1972 and functioned for barely an hour before permanently shutting down.

⊛ 1-61   So that's what happens when you move two light minutes closer to the Sun. Travel farther out and the problem becomes not heat but cold, as Mars frigidly proves. It, 35 too, was once a much more congenial place, but couldn't retain a usable atmosphere and turned into a frozen waste.

1 下線部（1）のように言える理由を、以下の2点について第1段落の内容に即して日本語でまとめなさい。

the right distance: ....

....

the right sort of star: ....

....

2 下線部（2）の意味するところを、本文に即して日本語で説明しなさい。

....

....

....

3 下線部（3）に関し、Venus のその具体的内容を下の4要素について簡潔に日本語で述べなさい。

水 ： ....

CO_2: ....

温度： ....

気圧： ....

4 次の英語の質問に、60字以内の日本語で答えなさい。句読点も1字に数えます。　　　　　　(大阪府立大)

According to the third paragraph, how have we obtained the knowledge of Venus's surface?

5 本文の内容と一致するものを1つ選びなさい。

① It is predicted that our sun will have burned itself in ten million years rather than ten billion years.

② Recent researches have shown that Michael Hart's calculations were much more refined and accurate than they were once thought.

③ In spite of the similarity in size and composition, Earth and Venus differ greatly in surface temperatures and atmospheric pressure.

④ If Earth had been 5% closer to or 15% farther from the Sun, according to the latest studies, it would have been a more habitable planet with no greenhouse gases.

⑤ The closeness to the Sun once made Mars a comfortable planet for the survival of life.

Chapter 8

Overflowing with more information than we can possibly hold in our heads, we're ⊙ 1-66 increasingly handing off the job of remembering to search engines and smartphones. Google is even reportedly working on eyeglasses that could one day recognize faces and supply details about whoever you're looking at. But new research shows that outsourcing★

5 our memory — and expecting that information will be continually and quickly available — is changing our memorizing habits.

Research conducted by Betsy Sparrow, an assistant professor of psychology at ⊙ 1-67 Columbia University, has identified (1)three new realities about how we process information in the Internet age. First, her experiments showed that when we don't know

10 the answer to a question, we now think about where we can find the nearest web connection instead of the subject of the question itself. For example, the question "Are there any countries with only one color in their flag?" prompted study participants to think not about flags but about computers.

A second revelation: when we expect to be able to find information again later on, ⊙ 1-68

15 we don't remember it as well as when we think it might become unavailable. (2)Sparrow's participants were asked to type facts into a computer — for example, "The space shuttle Columbia broke up during re-entry★ over Texas in February 2003." Half were told that their work would be saved; the rest were told that their words would be wiped out. Those who believed that the computer would store the information recalled details less well on

20 their own. Sparrow compares their situation to one we all experience in the real world: "Since search engines are continually available to us, we may often be in a state of not feeling we need to remember the information internally. When we need it, we will look it up." Sound familiar?

The researcher's final observation: the expectation that we'll be able to find information ⊙ 1-69

25 regularly leads us to form a memory not of the fact itself but of where we'll be able to find it. "We are learning what the computer 'knows' and when we should pay attention to where we have stored information in our computer-based memories," Sparrow concluded in her report. "We are becoming closely related to our computer tools."

Before you grow nervous about turning into a cyborg★, however, you should know

30 that this new relation with our digital devices is really just a variation of a much more familiar phenomenon, what psychologists call (3)transactive memory. This is the unspoken arrangement by which groups of people give memory tasks to each individual,

with information to be shared when needed. In a marriage, one parent might remember the kids' afterschool appointments while the other keeps track of the recycling pickup schedule. In a workplace team, one member may deal with data and calculations while a colleague is charged with remembering client preferences.

1-70   The way we assign tasks to our computers is simply an extension of this principle — an instance of transactive memory carried out on a very grand scale. But (4)<u>this handoff</u> comes with a disadvantage. Skills like critical thinking and analysis must develop in the context of facts: we need something to think and reason about, after all. And these facts can't be Googled as we go; they need to be stored in the original hard drive, our long-term memory. Especially in the case of children, "(X) must precede (Y)," says Daniel Willingham, a professor of psychology at the University of Virginia, meaning that the days of drilling the multiplication table★ and memorizing the names of the Presidents aren't over quite yet. Adults, too, need to recruit a supply of stored knowledge in order to situate and judge new information they encounter. (5)<u>You can't Google context.</u>

★ outsourcing「外部に仕事を依頼すること」 re-entry「(宇宙船の大気圏への) 再突入」 cyborg「サイボーグ」 multiplication table「九九の表」

1 下線部 (1) に関し、新事実 3 点の内容を本文に即してそれぞれ日本語で簡潔に述べなさい。

- ....
....
- ....
....
- ....
....

2 下線部 (2) に関し、この人たちが受けた実験の内容とその結果を、本文に即して日本語で簡潔に述べなさい。

実験の内容：..
....

実験の結果：..
....

3 下線部 (3) の内容を 40 字以内の日本語 (句読点を含む) で述べなさい。

次ページへ続く→

4 下線部 (4) が指すところを本文中からそのまま抜き出しなさい。 (学習院大)

- -

5 空所 (X) (Y) に入る語句の最も適切な組み合わせを 1 つ選びなさい。

① (X) factual knowledge   —   (Y) stored information
② (X) factual knowledge   —   (Y) skill
③ (X) skill   —   (Y) factual knowledge
④ (X) critical thinking   —   (Y) skill

6 下線部 (5) の意味に最も近いものを 1 つ選びなさい。 (学習院大)

① You can't analyze context on the Internet.
② You can't use Internet information out of context.
③ You can't rely on the Internet because it gives false context.
④ You can't find context on the Internet.

7 本文の内容と一致するものを 1 つ選びなさい。 (学習院大)

① We are often annoyed by too much information from the Internet.
② Skillful use of the Internet helps us understand the world.
③ Memorizing facts is necessary to develop critical thinking.
④ Adults need not remember facts as much as children do.

Memo

Chapter 9

Charles Darwin had more in common with chimpanzees than even he realized. ◈2-1
Before he was universally known for his theory of natural selection, the young naturalist
made a decision that has long been praised as the type of behavior that fundamentally
separates humans from other apes.

5　　In 1858, before Darwin published *On the Origin of Species*, his friend Alfred Russel ◈2-2
Wallace mailed Darwin his own theory of evolution that closely matched what Darwin
had secretly been working on for more than two decades.　Instead of racing to publish
and ignoring Wallace's work, Darwin included Wallace's outline alongside his own
abstract★ so that the two could be presented jointly before the Linnean Society★ the
10　following month.　"I would far rather burn my whole book than that Wallace or any man
should think that (1)I had behaved in a paltry★ spirit," Darwin wrote.

This kind of behavior, seeking to benefit others and promote cooperation, has now ◈2-3
been found in chimps, the species that Darwin did more than any other human to
connect us with.　In the study, published in a major scientific journal, primatologist★
15　Frans de Waal and his colleagues presented chimps with (2)a simplified version of the
choice that Darwin faced.

Pairs of chimps were brought into a testing room where they were separated only by ◈2-4
a wire mesh.　On one side was a bucket containing 30 tokens★ that the chimpanzee could
give to an experimenter for a food reward.　Half of the tokens were of one color that
20　resulted in only the chimpanzee that gave the token receiving a reward. The other tokens
were of a different color that resulted in both chimpanzees receiving a food reward.　If
chimpanzees were motivated only by selfish interests, they would be expected to choose
a reward only for themselves (or it should be 50-50 if they were choosing randomly).
But individuals were significantly more likely to choose the cooperative option.

25　De Waal says that (3)previous studies showing chimps to be selfish may have been ◈2-5
poorly designed.　"The chimps had to understand a complex food delivery system," De
Waal wrote, "and were often placed so far apart that they may not have realized how
their actions benefited others."　De Waal added that his study does not rule out the
possibility that chimpanzees were influenced by reciprocal exchanges outside the
30　experimental setting such as grooming★ or social support.

(4)This latter possibility offers exciting research opportunities for the future. ◈2-6
Chimpanzee society, like the greater scientific community that studies them, is built

around such mutual exchanges. Science is a social activity, and sharing the rewards from one another's research allows scientists to improve their work over time. Like the chimpanzees he would connect us with, Darwin recognized the utility of (5)sharing rewards with others. ³⁵

> * abstract「概要、要約」 the Linnean Society「リンネ協会（博物学の定期刊行物を出版する英国の組織）」
> paltry「卑しい、けちな」 primatologist「霊長類学者」 tokens「代用コイン」 grooming「毛づくろい」

1 　下線部（1）に関し、"behave in a paltry spirit" とは具体的にはどんな行動を指すか、本文に即して日本語で説明しなさい。

....

....

2 　下線部（2）に関し、以下の質問に本文に即して答えなさい。

（ア）　チンパンジーに対して行われた実験においてチンパンジーにどのような「選択」が与えられたか、日本語で説明しなさい。

(九州大)

....

....

....

（イ）　その実験から得られた結果を、日本語で説明しなさい。

....

....

3 　下線部（3）を日本語に直しなさい。

....

4 　下線部（4）が指す具体的内容を日本語で説明しなさい。

....

....

5 　下線部（5）と同じ意味を表している英語2語からなるフレーズを文中から抜き出しなさい。

....

6 　本文の内容と一致するものを2つ選びなさい。

① 　Darwin decided to publish the outline of his friend Wallace's work along with his own.

② 　Darwin learned the benefits of mutual exchanges among scientists from his study on evolution.

③ 　De Waal suggested that the chimps in previous studies had been more selfish than those he used in his study.

④ 　In de Waal's experiments, the chimpanzees behaved in a distinctly clear pattern in the choice of the color of the tokens.

⑤ 　De Waal does not think that mutual exchanges among chimpanzees like grooming had an influence on the results of his experiments.

Should the government have more control over people's lives? Most people who are ◑2-11
advocates of democracy believe emphatically that the government should not. (1)Such
people believe that everyone should be free to make their own choices and live their lives
as they please and do so uninhibited by higher authorities. Recently, however, some
5 economists have argued that the government should play a greater role in people's lives.
These economists believe that governments can intervene in ways that greatly benefit
society and still protect basic democratic values.

In 2017, economist Richard Thaler received the Nobel Prize in Economics for his ◑2-12
work in the field of "behavioral economics." Thaler and his collaborators argued that
10 (2)traditional economic theories of how people behave are not fully accurate because they
fail to account for how people actually behave. They explain that traditional economic
theories are based on the belief that people act "rationally" and make all of their decisions
on the basis of what is best for them economically. On the contrary, Thaler's research
has shown that people do not, in fact, act "rationally" and instead make many choices
15 that are not the best in some aspects of life. For example, despite hundreds of scientific
studies showing that smoking cigarettes is unhealthy and dangerous, millions of people
continue to smoke. The reason people continue to smoke despite the harmful
consequences is because the effects of smoking are far away in the future. People may
become sick or die from smoking, but it will happen many years later. The effects are so
20 distant that smokers cannot perceive them now. Thaler's work has shown that if the
effects were more immediate, people would be more likely to avoid smoking.

Many behavioral economists like Thaler believe in an approach called "libertarian ◑2-13
paternalism." This means that governments and authorities should allow people to live
their lives as they please but that they should also give them incentives to do what is in
25 their best interest. In other words, (3)governments should "nudge" people to make better
choices. In fact, Thaler and his colleague Cass Sunstein published a book titled *Nudge:
Improving Decisions about Health, Wealth, and Happiness*. In this book, they provide many
examples of how governments, universities, and other institutions can "nudge" their
members to act in different (i.e. better) ways. For example, one study revealed that
30 people eat different foods depending on the order in which food is displayed to them. If
a cafeteria manager places unhealthy food before healthy food, people are more likely to
consume the unhealthy food. However, if he or she (4)does the opposite, diners will

choose the healthier options. Therefore, it is in the best interest of diners, cafeteria managers, and institutions to place healthy food before unhealthy food.

2-14　Thaler and Sunstein argue that governments and other institutions should be 35 required to adopt these policies in the best interest of society. They advocated for policies based on "libertarian paternalism" to achieve this.

2-15　The organization of food in a cafeteria is not a controversial issue. However, some people have challenged other aspects of "libertarian paternalism" by suggesting that it violates democratic principles of people's rights to choose what is best for themselves. 40 (5)These critics argue that requiring "libertarian paternalism" is unfair because it forces people to do things they would not otherwise do. The fact that such policies would be "paternalistic," meaning that they would require something, violates the "libertarian" aspect. For example, New York City politicians proposed a law that would prohibit the sale of soda larger than 0.47 liters. Since soda is unhealthy (it causes tooth problems, is 45 linked to weight gain, and can cause diabetes, among many other problems), politicians believed prohibiting the sale of large quantities of soda would help make their city population healthier. However, critics proclaimed that this went against democratic principles that declare people should have freedom to buy what they want. They argued, "If I want to buy a big soda, I should have the right to buy a big soda!" The soda policy 50 was ultimately abandoned, but its effect on politics still remains pertinent today.

2-16　Should the government adopt "libertarian paternalism" as a policy guideline? There is much ongoing debate concerning this proposal. Proponents believe it will make society better at a minimal cost, while opponents believe that it violates the basic principles of (A). Although the discussion continues, "libertarian paternalism" is 55 definitely worth considering as a possible policy solution to some of today's problems.

1 下線部（1）を日本語に直しなさい。

次ページへ続く→

2 第2段落の内容に関し、以下の2点について日本語で説明しなさい。

a) 下線部（2）に関し、Thaler たちはどのように批判しているか。

....

....

b) 下線部（2）に関し、Thaler の研究で何がわかったか。

....

....

3 下線部（3）の言い換えとして一番近いものを、次の中から1つ選びなさい。 （北海道大）
① government should lightly influence people to behave in more desirable ways
② government should secretly force people to make choices which will improve their lives
③ government should openly let people choose what they want to choose
④ government should forbid people to live as they like
⑤ government should gently encourage people to act paternally

4 下線部（4）の具体的な内容を英語で書きなさい。 （北海道大・改）

....

5 下線部（5）の理由について最も適切なものを、次の中から1つ選びなさい。 （北海道大）
① Without "libertarian paternalism," democracy could be harmful to people's right to choose.
② "Libertarian paternalism" lacks medical evidence for its plans to improve people's health.
③ "Libertarian paternalism" does not entirely protect people's freedom of choice.
④ There is too much freedom in democracy. Therefore, "libertarianism" is necessary.
⑤ "Libertarian paternalism" misses the fact that soda is actually unhealthy to some people.
⑥ Democratic principles, which include freedom, contradict the "libertarian" aspect in the notion of "libertarian paternalism".

6 空欄（A）に入る最も適切な1語を文中から選び、英語で答えなさい。 （北海道大）

....

Memo

The COVID-19 pandemic★ has rendered the behavior of most Americans ◉2-21 unrecognizable. Handshakes have turned into elbow bumps★. School and work are conducted remotely. Socializing happens (a). And now even our faces are becoming nearly unrecognizable as we don★ a mask in order to go out.

5　　　Outside of an operating room or a bank robbery, masks are not the norm★ in Western ◉2-22 countries. At times, face coverings, whether women's veils or bandanas worn by demonstrators, have sparked outright★ bans. In some parts of the U.S. during the pandemic, the requirement to put on a mask has brought about political protests, arrests and even (b). A security guard in Michigan was killed after telling a customer to put
10　on a mask. Even for the large majority of Americans who are willing to follow public health guidelines, masks have been an adjustment. They can be hot and uncomfortable. They impede★ communication and cover (1)identifying features in a way that gloves do not. They feel, well, weird★.

　　　But (2)weird behaviors can become standard, and long-standing customs can change, ◉2-23
15　behavioral scientists say. Half a century ago the idea that dog owners should pick up their pet's waste was so controversial that in New York City one prominent figure in the debate had a plastic bag of droppings★ thrown in her face at a public meeting. Yet pooper-scooper★ laws are now in place in cities large and small. Once upon a time, when buying an airline ticket or booking a table at a restaurant, travelers had to choose between
20　the smoking and nonsmoking sections. Today in most of the U.S., there is no such thing as a smoking section.

　　　To bring about such change, a new behavior must first ascend to the status of a social ◉2-24 norm. Norms include both the perception of how a group behaves and a sense of social approval or censure★ for violating that conduct. "(3)The critical thing to lock in that
25　norm is that you believe that other people expect you to do it," says behavioral economist Syon Bhanot of Swarthmore College. That expectation already exists in places such as hard-hit New York City, where those without masks are sometimes berated★.

　　　The point is that masks do not just protect the wearer, they protect others. Such ◉2-25 community-minded thinking fits with collectivist cultural norms in some parts of Asia,
30　where masks are routinely worn when one is sick — and where there is more experience with serious epidemics★. Even in the more individualistic U.S., protecting others can serve as a powerful motivator. (4)In an effort to determine what message would

encourage doctors to improve their handwashing habits, a study found that signs near hospital sinks reminding them to protect patients by washing their hands were more effective than ones reminding them to protect themselves. 35

2-26　　Similarly, the first wave of evidence about the harms of smoking focused on damage to the smokers themselves and had no effect on smoking in public spaces. People thought individuals had "the right to harm themselves," says psychologist Jay Van Bavel of New York University. "It really started to change once we realized the consequences of secondhand smoke. Do you have a right to damage kids at school, your colleagues at 40 work or the staff at a restaurant?" So far 28 states and Washington, D.C., have said the answer is (c) and passed comprehensive smoke-free-air laws.

2-27　　"Social norms can change rapidly," says social psychologist Catherine Sanderson of Amherst College, "and it doesn't take everybody." In (5)an online experiment conducted by researchers at the University of Pennsylvania, subjects engaged in social coordination 45 to assign names to an object. The tipping point★ for achieving enough critical mass to initiate social change proved to be just 25 percent of participants. "They become the social influencers, the trendsetters," Sanderson says.

2-28　　Leadership is critical, however, which is (d) behavioral scientists were so alarmed by the recent examples of Vice President Mike Pence and President Donald Trump 50 refusing to wear masks during public appearances. "They are the primary people who are setting norms, especially when it's on television or in the news," Van Bavel says. Those politicians are flouting★ the advice of their own public health officials. In early April the Centers for Disease Control and Prevention officially recommended "wearing cloth face coverings in [A] settings where other social distancing measures are difficult 55 to maintain." It did not help, however, that the new recommendation conflicted with earlier statements from officials suggesting that masks were ineffective or should be left for medical professionals, who needed them more.

2-29　　The pro-mask★ message has become more consistent just a few weeks later. Multiple studies show the benefits of masks. One from statistical researchers at Arizona State 60 University found that (6)if 80 percent of the population adopted even only moderately effective coverings, the practice would prevent as much as 45 percent of projected deaths in New York State and reduce fatality numbers by up to 65 percent in Washington State. Absent virtuous role models at the national level, state, local and private institutions, as well as celebrities, have begun to exert their considerable power to bring about change. 65 "People are putting pictures of themselves in masks as their profile pictures," Bhanot says. Airlines and universities are requiring anyone who boards a plane or comes on campus to wear a mask. "As that gets scaled up to all elements of society, you will have greater compliance," Van Bavel says.

Barriers remain. The politicization* of masks in the U.S. might mean that some areas of the country will never adopt them entirely. And endemic* racism has led some young black men to fear that they will be mistaken for criminals if they wear masks in stores.

Once masks become the norm in most places, however, donning them will not seem odd or alarming, says psychologist Alexander Todorov of Princeton University, who studies facial expression. "People compensate. When they meet on the street, there is more gesticulation*. People engage in strategies to make sure that they're being (e)."

In truth, the adoption of masks is happening at a surprising pace. "The vast majority of people have, in a period of a few weeks, completely changed their (f) in radical ways," Van Bavel says. "In a year or three or five years, it might be more normal during flu season to see Americans or people from Western Europe wear masks. This might be what changes the norm."

* pandemic「世界的の流行病（の）」 bump「突き当てること」 don：to put on norm：standard
outright：complete and total impede：to delay or prevent someone or something by obstructing them
weird：odd, strange droppings「動物の糞（ふん）」 pooper-scooper「犬の糞をすくうシャベル」
censure：severe disapproval berate：to criticize angrily epidemic「流行病（の）」
tipping point「転換点、臨界点」 flout：to disregard openly, scorn
pro-mask：supporting the use of masks
politicization：making someone or something political in character endemic：deeply rooted
gesticulation：making gestures

1 空所 (a) ～ (f) に入る最も適切な単語を次の中から選びなさい。　　　　(大阪市立大)

①　understood　②　vividly　　　③　advised　　　④　why　　　⑤　calmness

⑥　how　　　　⑦　habits　　　　⑧　virtually　　　⑨　no　　　　⑩　violence

⑪　nothing　　⑫　expressions

2 下線部 (1)、(3) それぞれの言い換えとして最も適切な表現を選びなさい。　　(大阪市立大)

(1)　①　facial expressions which one can feel sympathy with

　　②　facial characteristics by which one can recognize people

　　③　facial characteristics that can attract others

　　④　facial points that are subject to the weather

(3)　①　The important thing to establish that norm

　　②　The dangerous thing to make that norm firm

　　③　The necessary thing to do without that norm

　　④　The essential thing to change that norm

3 下線部（2）の具体例を2点、第3段落の内容に即してそれぞれ日本語で簡潔に説明しなさい。

・

・

----

4 下線部（4）を日本語に直しなさい。 （大阪市立大・改）

----

5 下線部 (5) に関し、実験の結果からわかったことを、本文に即して日本語で簡潔に説明しなさい。

----

6 空所 [A] に入る最も適切な1語を本文中から選び、書きなさい。 （大阪市立大）

----

7 下線部（6）を日本語に直しなさい。 （大阪市立大）

----

8 本文の内容と一致するものを1つ選びなさい。

① At the beginning of the COVID-19 pandemic there were some protests against wearing masks, but most Americans were willing to wear them because it was a long-standing custom.

② A psychologist says that in individualistic countries like the U.S., it is not leadership but everybody's participation that can start to change social standards.

③ Many Americans have adopted wearing masks in public, but this is not the first time in America that a social behavior that was once a controversial issue became the standard behavior.

④ Since the start of the pandemic, the U.S. public health officials have been giving a consistent message about mask-wearing and its effectiveness.

⑤ After 25 percent of American people began to wear masks, the practice spread very rapidly, and in the future it might become the national norm during the flu season.

Chapter 12

Computer programs have reached a difficult point in their long journey toward ◎2-37 artificial intelligence (AI). They surpass people at tasks such as playing poker or recognizing faces in a crowd. Meanwhile, self-driving cars using similar technology run into pedestrians and posts and we wonder whether they can ever be reliable.

5　Among (1)these rapid developments and continuing problems, one essential building block of human intelligence has proven difficult for machines for decades: Understanding cause and effect.

Put simply, today's machine-learning programs can't tell whether a crowing chicken ◎2-38 makes the sun rise, or the other way around. Whatever volumes of data a machine
10　analyzes, it cannot understand what a human gets intuitively. From the time we are infants, we organize our experiences into causes and effects. (2)The questions "Why did this happen?" and "What if I had acted differently?" are what make us human, and so far are missing from machines.

Suppose, for example, that a drugstore decides to leave its pricing to a machine-learning ◎2-39
15　program that we'll call Charlie. The program reviews the store's records and sees that past variations of the price of toothpaste haven't correlated with changes in sales volume. So Charlie recommends raising the price to generate more revenue. A month later, the sales of toothpaste have dropped — along with dental floss, cookies and other items. (3)Where did Charlie go wrong?

20　Charlie didn't understand that the previous (human) manager varied prices only ◎2-40 when the competing stores did. When Charlie one-sidedly raised the price, price-conscious customers took their business elsewhere. The example shows that historical data alone tells us nothing about causes — and that the direction of causation is crucial.

Machine-learning systems have made surprising progress at analyzing data patterns,
25　but that is the low-hanging fruit of AI. To reach the higher fruit, AI needs a ladder, which we call the Ladder of Causation. Its steps represent three levels of reasoning.

The first step is Association, the level for current machines and many animals; on that ◎2-41 step, Pavlov's dogs learned to associate a bell with food. The next is Intervention: What will happen if I ring a bell, or raise the price of toothpaste? Intervention is different from
30　observation; raising the price one-sidedly is different from seeing what happened in the past. The highest step is (4)Counterfactual, which means the ability to imagine results, reflect on one's actions and assess other scenarios. Imagine giving a self-driving car this

ability. After an accident, its CPU would ask itself questions like: What would have happened if I had not honked at the drunken pedestrian?

2-42　　To reach the higher steps, machines need a model of the causal factors — essentially, 35 a mathematics of cause and effect. A simple element might be: "Liquor affects people's judgment, and that makes them move in unexpected ways." We can describe this using what scientists now call a causal diagram, in which arrows represent a series of possible causes: (5)Liquor ≫ Affected Judgment ≫ Unexpected Motion. Such diagrams enable the car to predict that certain pedestrians will react differently to the honking of its horn. 40 They also give us the possibility of "interrogating" the car to explain its process: Why did you honk your horn?

2-43　　Current machine-learning systems can reach higher steps only in areas where the rules are not violated, such as playing chess. Outside those areas, they are fragile and easily make mistakes. But with causal models, a machine can predict the results of 45 actions that haven't been tried before, reflect on its actions, and apply its learned skills to new situations.

1　下線部（1）を、本文中の例を用いて、具体的に日本語で説明しなさい。　　　　　　　（島根大）

....
....
....

2　下線部（2）を日本語に直しなさい。

....
....

3　下線部（3）について、Charlie の値段の決め方と人間の店主の値段の決め方の違いを、本文にそって日本語で説明しなさい。　　　　　　　（島根大）

....
....
....

4　下線部（4）の具体的内容を、本文にそって日本語で説明しなさい。

....
....
....

次ページへ続く→

5 下線部（5）の diagram が表している具体的内容を、本文にそって日本語で説明しなさい。

....

6 "cause and effect"を理解することによって、将来、機械がどのように進化すると考えられるか、本文にそって日本語でまとめなさい。

（島根大）

....

....

7 本文の内容と一致するものを 1 つ選びなさい。

① Computer programs are better than us at the task of recognizing faces in a crowd and that is why we think self-driving cars can be trustworthy.

② We cannot tell whether "a crowing chicken makes the sun rise" or "a chicken crows in response to the daylight" until we learn cause and effect later in our childhood.

③ Today's machine learning programs are on the level of Intervention, and can analyze human actions with causal reasoning.

④ If Charlie had known more about the previous record of the drugstore, the store wouldn't have lost customers to its rival stores.

⑤ Today's machine-learning systems haven't yet reached the level where they can predict the results of actions without having tried such actions before.

2-48   Social networks often stand accused of being enemies of productivity. According to one popular (if questionable) online source of information, the use of Facebook, Twitter and other such sites at work costs the American economy $650 billion each year. Our attention spans are weakening, our test scores declining, because of these "weapons of mass distraction." Yet (1)such worries have arisen before. In England in the late 1600s, similar concerns were expressed about another new media-sharing environment, the appeal of which seemed to be undermining young people's ability to concentrate on their studies and their work: the coffeehouse. It was the social-networking site of its day.

2-49   Like coffee itself, coffeehouses were an import from the Arab world. England's first coffeehouse opened in Oxford in the early 1650s, and hundreds of similar establishments sprang up across England in the following years. People went to coffeehouses not just to drink coffee, but to read the latest pamphlets and news-sheets, catch up on rumor and gossip, and talk to other coffee drinkers, both friends and strangers. Some coffeehouses were used as post offices, and (A)patrons would visit their favorite coffeehouses several times a day to check for mail. Some coffeehouses specialized in discussion of particular topics, like politics, literature or business. As customers moved from one shop to another, information circulated with them in wide-ranging conversations. (2)One reason these conversations were so lively was that social distinctions were not recognized within coffeehouse walls. Patrons were not merely permitted but encouraged to strike up conversations with strangers from entirely different walks of life.

2-50   Not everyone was pleased. Critics worried that coffeehouses were keeping people from productive work. But rather than functioning as enemies of industry, coffeehouses were in fact hotbeds of creativity because of the way in which they facilitated the mixing of both people and ideas. Members of the Royal Society, England's pioneering scientific society, frequently retired to coffeehouses to extend their discussions. It was a coffeehouse argument among fellow scientists that spurred Isaac Newton to write his foundational works of modern science.

2-51   Coffeehouses were platforms for innovation in the world of business, too. Merchants used coffeehouses as meeting rooms, which gave rise to new companies and business models. A London coffeehouse called Jonathan's, where merchants kept particular tables to transact business, turned into the London Stock Exchange. Lloyd's coffeehouse, a popular meeting place for ship captains, ship-owners and traders, became the well-

known insurance market. And the economist Adam Smith wrote much of his masterpiece *The Wealth of Nations* in the British Coffee House, a popular meeting place for Scottish
35 intellectuals, among whom he circulated early drafts of his book for discussion.

[　a　] there was some time-wasting going on in coffeehouses. But their merits far ⊙2-52 outweighed their drawbacks. (3)Now the spirit of the coffeehouse has been reborn in our social-media platforms. They, too, are open to all comers, and allow people from different walks of life to meet, debate, and share information with friends and strangers alike,
40 making new connections and sparking new ideas. Such conversations may be entirely virtual, but they have enormous potential to bring about change in the real world. Progressive companies are embracing "enterprise social networks" to encourage collaboration, discover hidden talents and knowledge among their employees, and reduce the use of e-mail. A recent study found that use of social networking within companies
45 increased productivity by 20 to 25 percent. The use of social media in education, meanwhile, demonstrates that students learn more effectively when they interact with other learners. There is always an adjustment period when new technologies appear. During this transitional phase, which can take years, technologies are often criticized for disrupting existing ways of doing things. But what we understand from the coffeehouse
50 is that modern fears about the dangers of social networking are (B)overdone. As we grapple with the issues raised by new technologies, there is much we can learn from the past.

1 下線部（1）に関し、以下の2点について第1段落の内容に即して日本語で説明しなさい。

（1）「このような懸念」とは何か。

....
....

（2）「以前に生じた懸念」とは何だったか。

....
....

2 下線部（2）を日本語に直しなさい。

....
....

3 以下の2点について、本文に書かれていることを日本語で簡潔にまとめなさい。

(1) coffeehouse と Isaac Newton の関係

....

....

(2) coffeehouse と the London Stock Exchange の関係

....

....

4 下線部（3）の内容を最も端的に述べた1文を同じ段落内から探し、その文を日本語に直しなさい。

....

....

....

5 下線部（A）（B）の語について、それぞれの質問に答えなさい。

(A) 同意語を同じ段落内から1語抜き出しなさい。

(B) 最も意味の近い語を1つ選びなさい。

① reasonable　　② excessive　　③ passed　　④ rational

6 In the context of the passage, choose the best answer for each question. （慶應義塾大）

(1) **Choose the best expression to fill in the blank [a].**

① Similarly　　② No doubt　　③ Rarely　　④ Suspiciously

(2) **What is NOT a role of social networks today?**

① To increase the productivity of workers who discuss company policies and practices.
② To expose users to a wide range of issues, from science to politics and literature.
③ To make connections with others who are trying to solve similar problems.
④ To discover hidden information from employees who work at rival companies.

(3) **Which is true for both coffeehouses and online networks?**

① Existing ways of doing business promote innovations that bring change.
② It is easy to distinguish the different cultural backgrounds of people.
③ There are opportunities for coming into contact with interesting ideas.
④ Public institutions like the post office are being hurt by online transactions.

(4) **What is the most appropriate title for the passage?**

① The Unrecognized Influence of Arab Culture on British Society
② The Surprising Diversity of Coffeehouses in English History
③ The Lesson of Coffeehouses for Online Social Networks
④ The Enemy of Productivity for Developing Businesses Today

Growing evidence that countries where there is more inequality of income are ⊕2-57 places where there is less equality of opportunity helps us understand why the United States has become one of the advanced countries with the least equality of opportunity. A young American's life prospects are more dependent on the income and education

5 of his parents than those of young people in other advanced nations.

Inequities in access to education are among the reasons the United States is no longer the land of opportunity. Even more disastrous is how education perpetuates advantages and disadvantages: of Americans born around 1980, only about 9 percent of those from the bottom quarter of the income distribution graduated from college.

10 One reason for (1)this is the cost of higher education.

And in the United States, "justice for all" is supposed to be its slogan. Yet ⊕2-58 increasingly, America is more appropriately described as offering "justice for those who can afford it." The rule of law is supposed to protect the weak against the strong. And it is supposed to mean that the law is (2)impartially enforced. We have

15 laws that are designed to protect people from unjust takings of their property. But we didn't enforce the laws against the bankers — not a single one went to jail for the gross miscarriage of justice* in the financial crisis of 2008.

Earlier I described America's high level of inequality of opportunity. A large ⊕2-59 fraction of Americans — those that weren't lucky enough to be born of parents of

20 means — have little chance of living up to their potential. (3)This is, of course, a disaster for these individuals, but it is also bad for the economy: we are not using fully our most important resource, our people.

As a government of the 1 percent, for the 1 percent, and by the 1 percent works to enrich the 1 percent, through welfare and tax benefits, fewer resources are available

25 for investments in infrastructure, education, and technology, investments that are needed to keep the economy strong and growing.

But the real cost of inequality is to our democracy and our society. Basic values ⊕2-60 for which the country has stood — equality of opportunity, equal access to justice, a sense of a system that is fair — have been eroded. A tax system such as ours is, for

30 instance, based on voluntary compliance. It works if there is a belief that the system is fair — but (4)it is now evident to all that ours is not, that those at the top get a far better deal than those in the middle.

As in so many other instances, when troubles emerged, the financial sector demanded to be paid back first — putting the welfare of ordinary citizens, including workers with contracts promising them retirement benefits, (5)in the backseat.

³⁵

No society can function without trust. Although economists typically don't use words like "trust," in fact, our economy simply can't function without trust. And inequality has eroded this most precious thing, and (6)once eroded, it may be hard to restore.

　　*　miscarriage of justice「誤審」

1 下線部（1）が指している部分を日本語に直しなさい。 (早稲田大)

------

2 下線部（2）の意味に最も近いものを 1 つ選びなさい。 (早稲田大)

① partly　　② unequally　　③ without favoritism　　④ with prejudice

3 下線部（3）が指す内容を日本語に直しなさい。

------

4 下線部（4）を、ours is not の内容を明らかにしながら日本語に直しなさい。

------

5 下線部（5）の意味に最も近いものを 1 つ選びなさい。 (早稲田大)

① in a neutral place　　　　　② in an important place
③ in a privileged place　　　　④ in second place

6 下線部（6）を、it の指すものを明らかにしながら日本語に直しなさい。

------

7 本文の内容と一致するものを 1 つ選びなさい。

① Young people in the United States are more financially independent of their parents, compared with those in other advanced nations.

② In the financial crisis of 2008, the American slogan "justice for all" was rightly applied to the poor as well as the wealthy, as it is supposed to be.

③ More investments are necessary in human resources than in infrastructure, education, and technology to keep the American economy strong and growing.

④ Preferential treatment given to the richest 1 percent of the population will widen inequality in the United States and will also threaten its democracy.

Chapter 15

The first commercially available digital camera was launched in 1990. In the decade ⊛2-66 that followed, it created a lot of anxiety in photographers and photography scholars. Some went as far as declaring photography dead as a result of this shift. Initially this was considered too steep a change to be classified as a reconfiguration*, rather (1)it was seen as a break. A death of something old. A birth of something new.

Digital images can also be easily copied, duplicated and edited. The latter made the ⊛2-67 flexibility of what photos can be seen as representing more obvious. It also made representing ourselves and our lives easy, cheap and quick. Additional shots now come with no additional costs, and we can and do take 10, 20, 30 snaps of any given thing to sort through later. In addition to transforming the individual value of the image, (2)this has altered the emotional meanings we attributed both to keeping and getting rid of individual photographs. Printed images of loved ones used to be kept even if they were out of focus, blurry or had development mistakes on them. In the context of the massive amount of digital images, the labour of love now becomes the cleaning, sorting, tagging, categorizing and deleting majority of the photos. While it is occasionally claimed that this emergent acceptance of deleting photos is indicative of their diminished social worth, there are plenty of digital snapshots that are printed out, displayed as the lock-screen on devices, or used as the background of the computer screen. Overall, we can say that digitalization has shifted the focus of photography from photographs themselves to the act of taking pictures.

The first camera phones date back to the very beginning of the twenty-first century. ⊛2-68 In early 2001, the BBC reported on the first cell phone with a camera invented in Japan. Readers from around the world offered their ideas on what such a peculiar invention might be good for. Some said it could have many uses for teenagers (streamlining shopping for outfits, proving you have met a pop idol, setting up your friends on dates) but would be pretty pointless for adults. Others thought it would be a practical aid for spying, taking sneak pictures of your competitors' produce or quickly reporting traffic accidents and injuries. (3)Yet others thought it might be nice for travelers to keep in touch with their families or hobbyists to show art or collections to others. My personal favourites include commenters who wrote they couldn't wait for the device to be available at a reasonable price in their home country, so they can take pictures of the friendly dogs they meet at the park. Someone suggested the camera needs to be on the front to allow for video calls, which didn't happen in practice until 2003.

2-69 A digital culture scholar claims that the fact that we always carry a camera alters what can be and is seen, recorded, discussed and remembered. Some photography scholars 35 propose that camera phones and camera phone images have three social uses — to capture memories, to maintain relationships, and to express yourself. (4)In contrast, another scholar argues that the camera phone is no different from other portable image making devices and that the uses and meanings attributed to home videos in the 1980s have been exactly the same — memory, communication and self-expression. In this 40 sense, the social function of photography seems to have remained despite the changes through various reconfigurations of technology and cultural imaginaries about it.

　* reconfiguration = modification; redesign

1 下線部（1）の意味を、it の指すものを明らかにしながら、本文に即して日本語で説明しなさい。

----

2 下線部（2）は具体的にどのようなことを指しているか、本文に即して日本語で説明しなさい。　　　（京都大）

----

3 下線部（3）を日本語に直しなさい。　　　（京都大）

----

4 下線部（4）を日本語に直しなさい。

Chapter 16

Rumours spread by two different but overlapping processes: popular confirmation ⊕ 2-74 and in-group momentum. The first occurs because each of us tends to rely on what others think and do. Once a certain number of people appear to believe a rumour, others will believe it too, unless they have good reason to think it is false. Most rumours involve topics on which people lack direct or personal knowledge, and so most of us often simply trust the crowd. As more people accept the crowd view, the crowd grows larger, creating a real risk that large groups of people will believe rumours even though they are completely false.

In-group momentum refers to the fact that when like-minded people get together, ⊕ 2-75 they often end up believing a more extreme version of what they thought before. Suppose that members of a certain group are inclined to accept a rumour about, say, the evil intentions of a certain nation. In all likelihood, they will become more committed to that rumour after they have spoken to each other. (1)Indeed, they may move from being tentative believers to being absolutely certain, even though their only new evidence is what other members of the group believe. Consider the role of the internet here: when people see many tweets or posts from like-minded people, they are strongly inclined to accept a rumour as true.

(2)What can be done to reduce the risk that these two processes will lead us to ⊕ 2-76 accept false rumours? The most obvious answer, and the standard one, involves the system of free expression: people should be exposed to balanced information and to corrections from those who know the truth. Freedom usually works, but in some contexts (3)it is an incomplete remedy. People do not process information in a neutral way, and emotions often get in the way of truth. People take in new information in a very uneven way, and those who have accepted false rumours do not easily give up their beliefs, especially when there are strong emotional commitments involved. It can be extremely hard to change what people think, even by presenting them with facts.

1 文中の popular confirmation および in-group momentum とは何か、それぞれ 30 字以内の日本語で述べなさい。

popular confirmation

									10					15

in-group momentum

									10					15

2 下線部（1）を日本語に直しなさい。

3 下線部（2）の問いに対し、人々はどうすべきだと述べているか、日本語で答えなさい。

4 下線部（3）のように述べている理由は何か、日本語で答えなさい。

5 英文の要旨を 70 〜 80 字の日本語にまとめなさい。（句読点も字数に含める）

（東京大）

									10										20

Chapter 1

テーマ解説

遺伝子工学は、あらゆる生物の細胞中にある遺伝子を研究・利用することによって、医療や食品など既存のさまざまな分野への応用を期待する、新しい学問分野である。

遺伝子は、DNA の遺伝情報を元に、その生物が正常に生命維持するために不可欠なタンパク質を複製する。遺伝子工学は、この遺伝情報の人工的な操作によって、本来その生物が持たない機能を与える。

例えば、ある薬剤を培養できる生物の遺伝子を操作することで、その薬剤を大量に安く培養（製造）できるようになった例がある。また、青果物の遺伝子を改良操作することで、耐虫性を持たせたり、よりおいしくしたり、より大量に実を結ばせたりすることができる。こうした一部の青果物は**遺伝子組み換え食品（GM [genetically modified] food）**としてすでに利用されている。

一方、遺伝子を操作することによる問題もある。生物兵器やヒトクローンは、倫理的・宗教的に物議を醸している。また、遺伝子を操作することによって、結果その生物にどのような悪性が生まれるかがわからないので、未知の危険は常につきまとう。

▶ 本文出典

イギリスの週刊科学雑誌 *NewScientist* 2009 年 1 月 7 日号に掲載された記事の冒頭を抜粋、一部調整したもの。

▶ DNA sequence

DNA 配列。4 種類の塩基（A：アデニン、C：シトシン、G：グアニン、T：チミン）の配列によって、DNA の遺伝情報が決定される。

©The Pennsylvania State University

マンモス

▶ woolly mammoth

「ケナガマンモス」と呼ばれることもあるが、日本人が一般的に認識している「マンモス」のこと。巨大な牙が特徴である。

▶ Stephan Schuster

1963-。ペンシルベニア州立大学の生化学・分子生物学教授。絶滅した種の化石や毛皮から DNA を復元する「ミュゼオミクス（museomics、同氏による造語）」の先駆者とされている。現在は、かつて北半球寒冷地に生息していた絶滅種であるケナガマンモスの遺伝子情報解析に注力している。この解析が終了すれば、およそ 10 億円でクローンを生み出せると主張している。

Lynn Tomsho, Penn State

スティーブン・シュスター教授

▶ Siberia

ロシア連邦の、ウラル山脈を含む東側の地域。一般的には極寒の地として知られる。

▶ Svante Pääbo

1955-。スヴァンテ・ペーボと読む。スウェーデン生まれの生物学者で、現職はマックス・プランク進化人類学研究所の遺伝学部門ディレクター。旧人類の DNA 解析により、現代の人類はネアンデルタール人の遺伝情報の一部を受け継いでいることを明らかにしたほか、旧人類の絶滅種であるデニソワ人を、科学史上初めて DNA の解析のみによって発見した。絶滅した種のゲノムから人類の進化を解明する取り組みが評価され、2022 年にノーベル生理学・医学賞を受賞した。

Foto: Frank Vinken

スヴァンテ・ペーボ博士

Chapter 2

テーマ解説

近年話題の**食事法（diet）**の１つに**グルテンフリー（gluten free）**というものがある。減量や健康維持に効果的とされており、グルテンを含む食品を摂らないようにすることを言う。グルテンとは、小麦に含まれる２種のタンパク質が水と結合したもので、麺やパンなどの小麦加工食品を作る際にかかせない。

グルテンには、**アレルギー症状（allergic symptoms）**を引き起こすおそれがある。小麦アレルギーを持つ人や、「セリアック病」（グルテンに対して、アレルギーよりもさらに過剰な免疫反応を引き起こす疾患）を持つ人にとって、グルテンフリーの食事は必須だ。また、グルテン過敏症などの「小麦に弱い」体質の人にとっても、消化器系の状態改善や倦怠感の緩和などが期待できる。加えて、グルテンには中毒性があり小麦製品の摂取を促しやすいため、グルテンフリーは減量手段として効果的だ。

このように、グルテンフリーは健康的な食事法として注目を集めているが、本当にメリットばかりなのだろうか。小麦食品の摂取を制限することは、そこから得られていたビタミンＢや食物繊維、ミネラルなどの栄養素も制限することを意味する。グルテンに対するアレルギーを持たない人がグルテンフリーを実施すると、栄養バランスが崩れ、かえって体調不良や肥満を引き起こすおそれがあるのだ。

メリットがあればその裏にデメリットが潜んでいることはよくある。表層的な部分だけでなく、隠された裏側にまで意識を配ることが肝要だ。

▶ 本文出典

Howard S. Friedma and Leslie R. Martin, *The Longevity Project: Surprising Discoveries for Health and Long Life from the Landmark Eight-Decade Study*, Plum, 2012.

Chapter 3

▶ 本文出典

Douglas Adams, "Cookies," *The Salmon of Doubt: Hitchhiking the Galaxy One Last Time*, Crown, 2003
（イギリスの作家、ダグラス・アダムズの遺稿集）

Chapter 4

テーマ解説

英語を**母語（first language）**とする国にイギリス・アメリカ・オーストラリアなどがある。その人口を足した数、すなわち英語を第一言語とする人は世界中で 3.5 ～ 4 億人程度といわれているが、この数は 10 億に及ぶ中国語母語者と比べて、多く見ても半数程度に過ぎない。

私たち日本人が国策として英語を学んでいるのは、その母語者と比べてはるかに多くの人々が、英語を**第二言語（second language）**、あるいは**公用語（official language）**として使用しているからである。英語を公用語とする国は 50 カ国以上、英語を外国語として使用する人は 20 億人を超える。これはすなわち、世界人口 70 億人のうち、その約 3 分の 1 は英語でコミュニケーションがとれるということを意味している。

歴史を振り返ってみれば、言語の広がりは侵略・支配の歴史と一致する。米国は北米東海岸を植民地とした英国から独立した国家であるし、オーストラリアは、もとは英国の流刑植民地であった。どちらも入植、支配した英国人が英語を広めたのである。

英語が現在の世界語として認められているのは、世界中のあらゆる面で非常に大きな影響力を持っている国が用いている言語だからである。誤解を恐れずに言えば、米国はあらゆる面で世界を支配しているのである。

▶ 本文出典

Laurie Bauer, Peter Trudgill, *Language Myths*, Penguin Books, 1999.

日本語の翻訳本は、『言語学的にいえば―ことばにまつわる「常識」をくつがえす』のタイトルで 2003 年に研究社から出版された。

本書は言語学者 21 人によるエッセイで構成されている。神戸大学の英文は責任編集者の１人である Peter Trudgill 氏の執筆による第 1 章 *The Meanings of Words Should Not be Allowed to Vary or Change* の一部。

Chapter 5

テーマ解説

視覚（sense of eyesight）に代表される**五感（five senses）**が生物にとって感覚的なのは、それが感覚的と判断されるまでに最適化され、使いこなされているからである。あらゆる感覚は、脳に届く生体信号によって知覚されるのであって、そのシステムを科学的に解明し、医療等に生かそうとする研究は近年ますます活発である。

生まれたときの鋭敏な感覚が加齢によって次第に衰えるのは、世間一般にも理解されている現象である。英国の企業が開発した Mosquitone という装置は、蚊の羽音のような不快な音を出す。この17キロヘルツの高周波数の音は、十代後半から二十代前半にしか知覚されず、たむろする若者を排除するのに利用されている。三十代以上の多くはこの音を知覚できない。年を取れば目も耳も悪くなるものだ。

加齢同様、生活環境が感覚に与える影響も大きい。アフリカで遊牧生活をする民族の視力は 8.0 に及ぶと言うし、小さなころから音楽に携わっている人の中には、いわゆる絶対音感という、秀でた能力を持つ人もいる。目が不自由な人は、訓練によって点字が読めるようになるし、また、音楽的に優れた才能を持つ人も多い。視覚の不自由によって聴覚や触覚が鋭敏になることもあり、後天的な要素も知覚には大きな影響を与えるとされる。感覚は、生活に応じて、脳が必要な情報とそうでない情報を取捨選択することによって、最適化されるのである。

▶ 本文出典

David Eagleman, *Incognito: The Secret Lives of the Brain*, Pantheon Books, 2011.

▶ Mike May

1954 年生まれ。本名 Michael G. May。妻と 2 人の息子がある。1984 年の冬季パラリンピック（オーストリア・インスブルック大会）において、スキー選手としてジャイアント・スラローム等の種目に出場し、3 つの銅メダルを獲得した。また、ダウンヒル種目において、全盲選手としては最速の時速 104 キロという記録を作ったこともある。音の反響で物の位置を判別する「エコーロケーション」と呼ばれる能力を持つと言われる。

2000 年、角膜と幹細胞の移植手術によって、部分的に視力を回復した。CIA やハイテクベンチャー企業で働いた経歴を持つが、近年はカリフォルニアでセンデロ・グループを設立、視覚障害を持つ多くの人々の雇用を生み出している。また、米スタンフォード大を中心とした視覚と脳の関係の研究にも参画している。

センデロ・グループのウェブサイトには、彼の紹介文とともに、多くの写真が掲載されている。
http://www.senderogroup.com/mm/mike.htm

▶ electro-chemical signals

電気化学的信号。

神経細胞（neuron）は、大まかに言って、核を持つ細胞体（cell body）と、情報を送り出す軸索（axon）からなる。細胞体の周囲には樹状突起（dendrites）があり、これは情報を受け取る役割をする。

樹状突起が化学物質による信号（chemical signals「化学信号」）を受信すると、細胞体は電気信号（electrical signals）を軸索に流し、それが軸索の末端にあるシナプス（synapses）に達する。しかし、シナプスと別の神経細胞の樹状突起の間には約 10 万分の 1 ミリの間隔があり、電気信号は伝わらない。その代わりに、シナプスは神経伝達物質と呼ばれる化学物質を分泌する。これが別の細胞体の持つ樹状突起にたどり着くと、再び電気信号が生じ、細胞体から軸索を通ってシナプスに伝わる。この一連の情報伝達が電気化学的信号と呼ばれるものである。

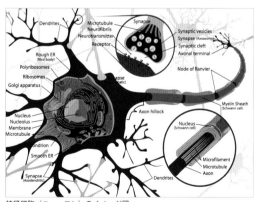

神経細胞（ニューロン）のイメージ図

Chapter 6

テーマ解説

「**地球温暖化（global warming）**」は、今や小学生でも知っている「常識」になった。「地球温暖化によって、**希少種（rare species）** が絶滅の危機に瀕している」「地球温暖化によって、世界中で**異常気象現象（abnormal weather phenomenon）** が増えている」「地球温暖化によって、低海抜の島が水没の危機にさらされている」といった論は大学入試英文の定番の1つであり、概ね「地球温暖化に対する懸念が表明」されていることが予想できるため、比較的取り組みやすいジャンルだといえるだろう。

地球温暖化が問題である最大の理由は、「人間以外の動植物が**絶滅（extinction）** するのは不憫だ」という感傷ではなく、我々人類が、予想される変化に対応するために莫大なコストを負担する可能性があるからである。各地域の社会は、その地域の気候に大きく依存している。つまり、地域経済はその地域で生産される農作物に依存し、地域社会はその地域に頻発する気象現象への備えを充実させてきたのだ。しかし、温暖化によって、農作物の生産量に深刻な影響をもたらす可能性があり、異常気象現象による被害が大きくなる可能性がある。

当然、より大きな被害を受けるのは、資金力と技術力に乏しい第三世界の人々である。**気候変動に関する政府間パネル（Intergovernmental Panel on Climate Change: IPCC）** の評価報告書によれば、地球温暖化が進んだ場合、農作物の収量が最も減少する可能性が高いのは、アジアやアフリカ、中南米の発展途上国が集中する**低緯度地域（low latitudes）** である。そうした国々は不足した食料を輸入する資金力が乏しいため、今以上の**飢餓（starvation）** が発生する可能性がある。

▶ 本文出典

Gabrielle Walker, David King, *The Hot Topic: How to Tackle Global Warming and Still Keep the Lights On*, Bloomsbury Publishing, 2008. を一部抜粋、一部改変したもの。

▶ the Central England Temperature Record

中部イングランド温度記録。1953年に英国の気候学者Gordon Manleyによってまとめられた、中部イングランド各地の気温データ。

〔参考〕 中部イングランド温度記録の月平均値と年平均値
MONTHLY MEAN CENTRAL ENGLAND TEMPERATURE (DEGREES C)

	JAN	FEB	MAR	APR	MAY	JUN
Year 1659	3.0	4.0	6.0	7.0	11.0	13.0
Year 1999	5.5	5.3	7.4	9.4	12.9	13.9
Year 2006	5.4	4.9	5.8	7.5	12.5	15.2

	JUL	AUG	SEP	OCT	NOV	DEC	AVR
1659	16.0	16.0	13.0	10.0	5.0	2.0	8.87
1999	17.7	16.1	15.6	10.7	7.9	5.0	10.65
2006	16.9	17.0	16.0	10.9	5.6	6.0	10.34

▶ the last ice age

最後の氷河期。約7万年前に始まり、1万年前に終了した氷河期で、地球全体の平均気温で比較すると、今よりも4～8℃ほど低かったと考えられている。この氷河期の中で最も寒かった時期は、陸上に降った雪がほぼ全て氷となって残ったため、海面は今よりも100メートルほど低かった。また、ヨーロッパ北部と北アメリカ大陸の北部は氷河で覆われていた。

Chapter 7

テーマ解説

よくよく考えてみれば、我々は自分がいまどこにいるのかということすら正確に知らない。宇宙はどのような場所か、地球は宇宙のどこにあるか、その絶対的な位置を正しく表す手段すら確立できていない。宇宙が人々を魅了してやまない理由も、その神秘性にあるのだろう。宇宙全体から考えれば塵にも及ばない地球、そこにいる人類は、ニュートンの時代から**観察（observation）** と**実験（experiment）** を続け、それに基づいた宇宙理論を作り上げてきた。しかしながら、宇宙は依然、その大半が謎のままである。宇宙は小さな「点」の大爆発によって始まったという有名な**ビッグバン理論（big bang theory）** も、現在では最も有力な説になってはいるものの、すべての**宇宙物理学者（astrophysicist）** に賛成されているわけではない。

遠くの星を見たとき、その光が何千年も前の星の姿を映していると聞いたことがあるだろう。このことを逆に考えれば、より遠くの宇宙を見れば、より古い宇宙を見られる、つまり、観測によって時間をさかのぼる、ということになる。どこまで遠くを見れば宇宙の創世を観測できるのか、そもそもそれが可能なのか。考えれば考えるほど謎は深まるばかりだが、これほど楽しい思索もそうあるものではないだろう。

▶ 本文出典

Bill Bryson, "Lonely Planet," *A Short History of Nearly Everything*, Broadway Books, 2003.

▶ Michael Hart

1932-。アメリカ生まれの宇宙物理学者。*The 100: A Ranking of the Most Influential Persons in History*（『歴史を創った100人』）の原著者としても有名。

▶ unmanned Soviet probe

旧ソ連が金星に送った探査機ベネラ・シリーズのうちの、ベネラ8号のこと。金星大気の調査を主目的に打ち上げられ、117日間かかって1972年7月22日に到着。大気中を下降中に風速を直接測定し、また金星表面が地球の曇天ほどの明るさであることなどを明らかにした。着陸後も、厳しい条件で破壊されるまで50分11秒にわたってデータ送信を続けた。

ベネラ8号

▶ light minute

光分。1分間に光が進む距離のことで、約1,800万キロメートル。1秒間に光が進む距離は地球を7周半＝30万キロメートル（地球は1周4万キロメートル）を基準に覚えておくとよい。

▶ Mars

火星。重力が地球に比べて半分以下のために、大気が希薄になり、よって熱が保たれない。平均気温はマイナス43℃と言われている。

NASA/JPL

火星。NASAによるこの画像では、氷雲、極氷や、極地などの地形的特徴が表されている。

Chapter 8

テーマ解説

　情報革命は人間の歴史上で4回あったと考えられる。最初の情報革命は今から約5,000～6,000年前の「文字の発明」、2回目は紀元前1,300年頃の「本の誕生」、3回目が15世紀半ばの「印刷技術の発明」、そして最後が現代の「インターネット革命」である。これら4つの情報革命は、いずれも情報が伝播する範囲を広げ、その速度を速めるものだった。

　中でも「印刷技術の発明」は昨今の「インターネット革命」と比較されることが多い。爆発的に印刷物が増加していった当初は、それが統制されることなく玉石混交の印刷物が氾濫していた。印刷物には間違いも多く、当時の編集者はそれを正すために、読者から広く間違いの指摘や批判を受け付け、次版への修正作業に生かしていたという。インターネットの特徴の1つといわれる**クラウドソーシング（crowdsourcing：不特定多数との共同作業）**と本質的にはなんら変わらないこうした発想が、16世紀には既に存在していたのである。さらに印刷物が増加する状況への批判も現代に通じるものがある。ある聖職者は「印刷会社は無数の本であふれさせ、人々の脳を無数の矛盾する見解で満たしている」と嘆き、「気まぐれで新しいものに惹かれがちな人々が古典を軽視している」ことを憂えていたのである。

　こうしたことを考えると、インターネット革命とは、人間が約600年前に経験したことの焼き直しに過ぎないという見方もあながち間違いではないようだ。人間は、こと情報に関しては本質的な部分では何も変わっていないということなのかもしれない。

▶ **本文出典**

　アメリカの雑誌 *Time* の2012年3月12日号に掲載された、Annie Murphy Paul 氏による記事 "Your Head Is In The Cloud" を改変したもの。

Chapter 9

テーマ解説

　チンパンジー（chimpanzee）や**オランウータン（orangutan）**などの類人猿とは違い、ヒトがこれほどまでに進化したのは、直立二足歩行がきっかけであると考えられている。両手が自由になったために道具を作ったり、火を使ったりすることができるようになった。また、脳の安定によってその容量が増え、口腔内の筋肉の発達によって高度な言語が使えるようになった — これがヒトの進化に関する一般的な**仮説（hypothesis）**である。

　ヒトはアフリカの類人猿の中から進化して誕生したものという仮説がある。いわゆるサバンナ説である。アフリカ大陸の気候変動によって食用植物がなくなり、住む地を変えたり、**狩猟（hunting）**による肉食に向かったりした。狩猟のために知恵を絞り、道具を作り、食べやすくするために火を使う — これらの説はヒトの進化を説明するにはもっともらしいものであるが、仮説の域を決して超えてはおらず、他にも有力な説はある。

　進化といえば、有名な**チャールズ・ダーウィン（Charles Darwin）**博士を思い浮かべるかもしれないが、彼の『進化論』にきっ抗する説が現在では多く論じられている。

▶ **本文出典**

　アメリカの月刊科学雑誌 *Scientific American* 2011年8月号に掲載された記事を短く調整し、改変したもの。
　オリジナルの英文は1,700語以上の長文で、本文にある実験の内容や結果が図表と共に詳細に記されている。

▶ **Charles Darwin**

　1809-1882。英国の自然科学者。『種の起源（*the Origin of Species*）』の筆者。現存する多様な生物種は、祖とする1つあるいはわずかな数の生物から、厳しい環境によって自然淘汰されながら進化したものだという「進化論」を提唱した。

▶ theory of natural selection

自然選択説（または自然淘汰説）。1859 年にチャールズ・ダーウィンとアルフレッド・ウォレスによって体系化された理論。生物に偶発的に発生する突然変異のうち生存環境に有利なものが生き残ることで、その種の進化の方向性が決まる、という考え方。

この理論を説明するとき、例としてキリンが取り上げられることが多い。
・かつては首が長いキリン、首が短いキリンが存在していた
・キリンの生存環境において、何らかの状況（例えば木の高いところからしか食料が入手できない状況）が発生し、首が短いキリンは生存できなくなった
・結果として首が長いキリンだけが生き残った
・その首の長さが遺伝され、その後は首が長いキリンだけが存在するようになった

▶ *On the Origin of Species*

『種の起源』。1859 年に出版されたチャールズ・ダーウィンの著作。正式な書名は *On the Origin of Species by Means of Natural Selection, or the Preservation of Favoured Races in the Struggle for Life*『自然選択、すなわち生存競争における有利な種の存続による、種の起原』。

『種の起源』の中では人類の起源については触れられていない。人間とサルの関係については、1871 年に発表された『人の由来と性選択（*The Descent of Man, and Selection in Relation to Sex*)』の中で、「人間はサルから進化したものでほぼ間違いないだろう」と記されている。

▶ Alfred Russel Wallace

1823-1913。英国の博物学者。地理的な要因が動物の分布に与えた影響について実地探査を繰り返し、1868 年にインドネシアにおける分布境界線（生物の分布の境界線）であるウォレス線を発見した。

▶ Linnean Society

リンネ協会。スウェーデンの生物学者で生物分類学の父と呼ばれるカール・リンネ（1707-1778）の標本を全て買い取った英国の富豪によって、1788 年、ロンドンに設立された学術組織。大英帝国博物館と並び英国の博物学研究において長く中心的役割を果たした。

Chapter 10

テーマ解説

　現代社会においては、人間の行動を変化させることが経済的にも社会的にも最大の関心事だろう。ビジネスの世界では「数ある中から自社商品を選択させる」ことが必要であり、政治や行政でも「社会の効率化」や「公衆衛生の向上」といった目的を達成するために市民の行動変容を促す必要があるからだ。人間の行動を変化させる古典的な手法は、「法の整備」**「金銭的誘因（monetary incentive）」**である。最も強制力がある手法は、法を整備することであるのは言うまでもない。さらに、「他社からの乗り換えで、基本料1年間無料」といった企業広告や、「時短営業に協力すれば、日額数万円を支給」といった行政からの「利得の提供」も多く見られる。

　そして、現在注目されているのは、人間の心理や行動の傾向を利用して「誘導」する手法である。例えば、数十に上るレストランのメニューの中の数品目に、目立つように「おすすめ」や「人気メニュー」といった表記を載せることである。さまざまな研究結果からこうした表記がある品目の売上は確実に向上することがわかっている。この事例は、行動経済学における**ナッジ（nudge：そっと後押しする）**と呼ばれる手法の事例としてよく取り上げられる。「法」や「金銭的誘因」と比較すると効果は薄いものの、多数の合意や追加コストの負担が不要なため、企業だけでなく行政などによって私たちが認知できないレベルで無数に採り入れられている。

　行動経済学の用語としてのナッジは、「人々が自身にとってより良い選択を自発的にとれるよう手助けするもの」と定義されている。つまり、手助け［誘導］される側が利益を得ることが前提である。しかし、誘導する側の利益を増大させることを目的とするもの、例えば、味の評価を度外視して最も利益率が高いメニューに「おすすめ」の表記を載せるといった「誘導」が多いのも現実だ。「誘導」に嫌悪感を持つ人が一定数存在するのは、誘導する側の目的が明確でないことが多いからである。

▶ **behavioral economics**

　行動経済学。経済学の1分野。2002年にノーベル経済学賞を受賞した心理学者のカーネマン Kahneman,D.、同じく心理学者のトベルスキー Tversky,A.、経済学者のセイラー Thaler,R.H. らによって創設された。人間は情報の影響を受けたり、直感や感情による判断や決定を行ったりするため、必ずしも合理的に行動しない。そのことに着目し、伝統的な経済学ではうまく説明できなかった社会現象や経済行動を、人間の行動や心理を観察することで実証的にとらえようとすることを目的としている。また、その結果市場や資源配分、所得分配、そして人びとの幸福度や満足度にどのような影響があるのかを研究する学問。

▶ **libertarian**

　自由至上主義者。リバタリアニズム（自由主義）を主張する人。自由主義とは、他社の自由を侵害しない範囲での個人的な自由、経済的な自由などあらゆる自由を尊重しようとする立場のこと。

　最初にリバタリアンという言葉が使われたのは、1789年の英国の歴史家ウィリアム・ベルシャムによるものだという記録がある。

Chapter 11

テーマ解説

　過去の悲惨な**感染症（infection）**による被害は、人の移動の拡大と強く結びついている。欧州に大きな被害をもたらした14世紀の**ペスト（black plague）**の流行は、モンゴル帝国の拡大によってアジア圏との人流が拡大したことが大きな要因だったと言われている。1918年に発生し、全世界での推計死者数が4千万人とも1億人とも言われる、いわゆる**スペイン風邪（Spanish flu）**という新型インフルエンザの流行の時代背景には、船舶や飛行機による広域移動活性化と第一次世界大戦による軍の広域移動があった。

　個人レベルでの感染症対策は、100年前にはほぼ確立されていた。スペイン風邪が日本で流行し始めた1919年1月に、当時の内務省衛生局は「流行性感冒（かぜ）予防心得」を公開している。そこには「たくさん人の集まっているところに立ち入らない」「咳やくしゃみをするときはハンカチ、手ぬぐいなどで鼻、口を覆う」ことなどが重要だと書かれている。「手洗い」にほとんど言及されていない点は異なるが、他は今の感染症対策とほぼ変わらないことに驚かされる。

　人の移動が感染拡大に大きく影響するのは明白だが、集団における感染の広がりについては現在でも未解明な部分が多い。2019年に発生した**新型コロナウィルス感染症（Covid-19）**は発生後、全世界に拡大しやがて収束した。その後一定期間の停滞期を挟んで再び感染は拡大し収束する、といった波を数回繰り返した。全世界で都市封鎖を含む人流抑制策を実施していたにもかかわらず、ある時期を境として感染が急拡大したり、感染拡大期に比べて大きく人の流れが減少していないにも関わらず、感染が急速に収束に向かうという現象が起きる理由は、明確には分かっていないのだ。

　医療の発達は感染症のリスクを低下させる一方、科学技術の発達による人の移動の高速化と広域化は、そのリスクを増加させる。2015年、マイクロソフト社の創業者ビル・ゲイツ氏は「今後の人類にとっての最大の脅威は、戦争ではなく感染症だ」と言ったが、それはあながち間違いではないかもしれない。

▸ behavioral scientists

　行動科学者。行動学とは、人間の行動の法則を体系的に究明することを目的とした学問で、1950年頃からアメリカを中心として発展した。社会学、心理学、人類学、精神医学などが関連する。

▸ collectivist

　集産主義者。集産主義とは、生産手段を国や社会の共同所有にし、消費を個人の自由にゆだねることによって社会全体の福祉のために生活状態を改善しようとする思想。

　集産主義は、ソ連における社会主義、ファシズム（独裁的政治活動）、ナチズム（ドイツ労働者党、通称ナチス党による独裁的政治主義）などの政権下で採用された。典型的な例として、ソ連の集団農場による集団化（Collectivization）が挙げられる。

▸ the Centers for Disease Control and Prevention

　アメリカ疾病予防管理センター。アメリカ合衆国ジョージア州に本部を持つ感染症対策の総合研究所。1946年創設。略称はCDC。国内・国内を問わず人々の健康と安全の保護を主導するアメリカ合衆国の政府機関。健康に関する様々な決定の根拠となる情報の提供と、疾病の予防や管理、健康増進活動などを中心に行っている。2020年2月には、新型コロナウイルス感染症感染拡大防止のため感染者に向けてのガイドラインを公表した。

Chapter 12

テーマ解説

　機械学習（machine learinig）とは、**人工知能（artificial intelligence: AI）**分野におけるデータ解析手段の１つである。機械が膨大な量のデータを解析（反復学習）することで、それらのデータに潜む傾向や特長を法則化し、その法則を用いることで「分類」や「予測」などのタスクを機械が自動的に行うことを言う。人工知能分野の著名な研究者であるアーサー・サミュエルは、機械学習を「明示的にプログラムすることなく、学習する能力をコンピューターに与える研究分野」と定義している。

　類似の用語である**ディープラーニング［深層学習］（Deep learning）**とは、数ある機械学習のうちの１つで、現在最も多く利用されている手法だ。その技術は、**自動運転車（self-driving car）**や医療機器、宇宙開発など様々な分野で使用されている。

▶ **本文出典**

　2018 年 5 月 18 日付で The Wall Street Journal に掲載されたエッセイ、"AI Can't Reason Why" を一部改変したもの。執筆者は、Judea Pearl と Dana Mackenzie。

Chapter 13

▶ **本文出典**

　2013 年 6 月 22 日のアメリカの新聞 *The New York Times* に掲載された Tom Standage 氏によるエッセイ "Social Networking in the 1600s" を一部変更したもの。

▶ **coffeehouse**

　コーヒーハウス。

　1650 年頃から、貿易商人がアラブ地域から持ち帰ったコーヒーを出す店がロンドンやパリに出現し始めた。その後コーヒーは大量に輸入されるようになり、それまで黒ビールとブドウ酒、水以外の飲み物を口にすることがなかった人々の間で流行するようになった。それに合わせてコーヒーハウスも増え、18 世紀初頭にはロンドンだけで2,000 店を超えていたと言われている。

▶ **Social-networking site**

　ソーシャル・ネットワーキング・サイト（SNS）。人と人のつながりを促進する、コミュニティ型のウェブサイトのこと。2004 年に Facebook が登場し、この名称の知名度が高まった。日本における SNS 利用者数は 2014 年時点で約 6,000 万人で、アクティブユーザー（1 か月間に 1 回以上利用するユーザー）はその 50 〜 55% と推定されている。

▶ **Jonathan's**

　ジョナサンズ・コーヒーハウス。1680 年に Jonathan Miles によって開かれたコーヒーハウス。株式の取引は王立取引所で行われていたが、増えすぎた仲介業者の数を制限するようになった。それに反発した業者たちがジョナサンズに集まり、株式の売買を始めるようになった。

Chapter 14

テーマ解説

グローバル化（**globalization**）は、世界の**格差**（**rich-poor gap**）を縮小するが、先進国の国内格差を拡大する。世界銀行によれば、1990 年時点で 1 日 1.9 ドル未満で生活する人は全世界で約 20 億人だったが、2012 年には約 9 億人にまで減少した。この減少に最も貢献したのは「**世界の工場（world's factory）**」となった中国の発展だが、それはグローバル化の恩恵だった。一方、先進国内の単純作業労働者は、**新興国（developing countries）**の賃金水準と競争を強いられることになる。グローバル化の旗振り役だった米国で格差が拡大するのは必然だったといえる。

　グローバル化によって米国全体の**富（wealth）**が増加しているにもかかわらず、以前よりも貧しくなった人々が増えていることが問題なのである。かつて米国は、ほぼ全ての時代で「親の世代よりも子の世代のほうが豊か」な国だった。しかし現在は、「自分の親よりも貧しくなる人々」が無視できないほど増加した国になったのだ。

　歴史的にみれば格差は常に存在し、その大半は**世襲（hereditary）**によって固定されていた。しかし多くの場合、その格差には根拠があった。例えば、中世の欧州で「**持てる者（haves）**」だった貴族には、戦地に赴く義務があった。自らの命を賭して「**持たざる者（have-nots）**」である大衆を守る義務を負うことが、その身分の根拠だったのだ。今の大衆が、税で賄われている**社会基盤（infrastructure）**を最大限利用して莫大な利益を得ているにも関わらず、税制の盲点をついた節税に励むグローバル企業や、経営に失敗しても莫大な報酬が約束される大企業経営者に対して、そうした「根拠」を見出しにくいのも当然だろう。

▶ **本文出典**

Joseph E. Stiglitz, *The Great Divide: Unequal Societies and What We Can Do About Them,* W. W. Norton & Company, 2015. を一部抜粋、一部改変したもの。

　筆者の Joseph E. Stiglitz（ジョセフ・E・スティグリッツ）は、2001 年にノーベル経済学賞を受賞した米国の経済学者。

▶ **the financial crisis of 2008**

　2008 年の金融危機。日本では「リーマンショック」と呼ばれるこの金融危機の概要は以下の通り。1990 年代後半から 2006 年まで米国の住宅価格は上昇を続けていた。それを受けて当時米国第 4 位の証券会社リーマン・ブラザーズ社は無審査の住宅ローンを拡販した。その結果、中・低所得者や中小企業は、住宅を転売して利益を得る目的で、過剰な借り入れをする状況になった。2006 年から 2007 年にかけて住宅価格は暴落（バブル崩壊）し、その住宅ローンの大半が不良債権化した結果、リーマン社は 2008 年 9 月に破綻した。リーマン社はその住宅ローンを他の金融商品と複雑に組み合わせた証券として全世界の金融機関や企業、個人に販売していたため、推定損失額 800 兆円に上る世界規模の金融危機に発展した。リーマン社の経営陣は破綻の数年前には危機を察知していたにも関わらず、破綻する年まで数十億円という莫大な報酬を受け取っていたことが判明し、大きな批判を浴びた。

▶ **a government of the 1 percent, for the 1 percent, and by the 1 percent**

　この表現は、第 16 代アメリカ大統領 Abraham Lincoln のゲティスバーグ演説（Gettysburg Address）を下敷きとしている。南北戦争（the Civil War）の激戦地の 1 つである Gettysburg で行われた戦没者墓地の開設式でのリンカーンの演説は 300 語未満の短いものだったが、米国では特別な意義を持つものとなり、今なお引用されることが多い。それを結ぶ言葉が "government of the people, by the people, for the people shall not perish from the earth"「人民の、人民による、人民のための政治が、この地上から消え去ることがないようにしようではありませんか」。

【参考】筆者はこの入試問題の原文で、この演説とその引用に関し以下のように言及している。

"Of the 1 Percent, by the 1 Percent, for the 1 Percent," evoking the lines of President Lincoln's famous Gettysburg Address, arguing that the real issue of the Civil War was to ensure "that the government of the people, by the people, for the people, shall not perish from the earth." Democracy, we now know, is more than periodic elections: in some countries, such elections have been used to legitimize essentially authoritarian regimes and deprive large parts of the citizenry of basic rights.

「1％の1％による1％のための」は、有名なリンカーン大統領のゲティスバーグ演説を想起させるが、この演説は南北戦争の真の問題は「人民の人民による人民のための政府が、地球上から消滅しないよう」保証することだと主張している。今日私たちが知っている通り、民主主義は単に定期的な選挙を意味するのではない。一部の国々では、そうした選挙が本質的に独裁的な政権を正当化し、国民の大多数から基本的人権を剥奪するために利用されてきたのだ。

Chapter 15

▶ **本文出典**

Katrin Tiidenberg, *Selfies: Why We Love (and Hate) Them*, Emerald Publishing, 2018. を一部抜粋、一部改変したもの。

▶ **the first commercially available digital camera**

世界で初めて市販化されたデジタルカメラは、1990 年に Dycam 社が発売した「Dycam Model 1」である。解像度は 320 × 240 ピクセルで、内蔵メモリに 32 枚までの画像を保存することが可能だった。ちなみに、市販品ではない世界で最も古いデジタルカメラは、当時 Kodak 社のエンジニアだったスティーブ・サッソン氏が 1975 年に開発した試作機だとされている。しかし、当時アナログカメラ市場の最大手企業だった Kodak 社の経営幹部は、「面白いが、完成したことを口外しないように」と彼を口止めし、デジタル化への投資を行わなかった。その後、Kodak 社は 2000 年代以降のデジタル化の技術開発に遅れを取り、2012 年に経営破綻することとなった。

▶ **the first camera phone**

一般に、現在のカメラ付き携帯電話のルーツは、2000 年 10 月にシャープが商品化し、翌月 J-PHONE 社（現ソフトバンク社）が発売した J-SH04 だとされている。当時、メールに写真を添付する「写メール」が可能だったのは J-PHONE 社だけであったため、このメールサービスとともに J-SH04 は業界に大きな影響をもたらした。

J-SH04

▶ **BBC**

英国放送協会。正式名称は British Broadcasting Corporation。イギリスの公共放送局。1927 年に設立され、1936 年には世界初のテレビ放送を開始したことでも知られている。

Chapter 16

テーマ解説

私たちの生活から悪い噂を切り離すことはできない。認めたくはないが、悪い噂を話したり、共有することはストレス発散の方法や、集団内の仲間意識を芽生えさせる手段の一つとして、日常的に存在している。

あまりに度が過ぎた噂（あるいは**デマ (false rumor)、誹謗中傷（defamation / libel / slander)**）を流すことは、名誉毀損や業務妨害などの対象になる可能性がある。おそらく、世間の大部分の人間が「それらは自分には無関係だ」と考えているだろう。しかし、**SNS (social networking service)** が発達し、昔に比べて個人による情報発信が容易に、そしてその影響度が大きくなった現代においては、そう断言し切れるものではないかもしれない。というのも、SNS 上で話題になっている悪い噂を「シェア」、「リツイート」しただけでも、名誉毀損などの罪に問われる判例が昨今増加しているからだ。自身が悪い噂の第一発信者でなくとも、また**匿名で (anonymously)** 噂の共有をしたとしても、損害賠償を請求される可能性がある。

「所詮ただの噂」、「冗談のつもり」などと安易な気持ちで情報を拡散することが、犯罪行為につながりうる。悪い噂を好んでしまうという私たちの本質は変化していないのに、情報化が進んだことで、悪い噂の及ぼす影響や伴う責任の大きさが想像以上に拡大しているのだ。たとえ、悪い噂に興味を引かれたとしても、一度立ち止まってそれが持つ危険性を考えてみても損はないだろう。

▶ **本文出典**

Cass R Sunstein, *On Rumours: How Falsehoods Spread, Why We Believe Them, What Can Be Done*, Penguin, 2011. を一部抜粋、一部改変したもの。

Memo

Memo

Memo

Cutting Edge
Orange

定価 700 円＋税

初刷発行：2025 年 1 月 25 日

編著者：小林義昌

株式会社 エミル出版

〒102-0072　東京都千代田区飯田橋 2-8-1
TEL 03-6272-5481　FAX 03-6272-5482

ISBN978-4-86449-158-7 C7082

Cutting Edge

Orange

Navi Book

Chapter 6: Climate change isn't ...   *Chapter 7: We are, to a ...*   *Chapter 9: Charles Darwin had ...*

Chapter 11: The COVID-19 ...   *Chapter 13: Social networks ...*   *Chapter 14: Growing evidence ...*

ÉMILE

● 本書の使い方 ●

◆【語句】

　意味が空欄になっているものは、すべて入試必出の「重要語句」です。分からなければ辞書を引いて、覚えるまで何度も確認しましょう。

　音声ダウンロードを活用して、語句の正しい発音を確認しましょう。聞き流しながら語句の意味が確認できるように、音声は「英語→日本語（の意味）」の順で収録されています。

◆【本文解説】

　入試頻出の、少し分かりにくい構文、文構造を解説しています。難しいと感じた文については、問題を全て解いたあとでこの解説を読んで確認しましょう。また、参考書や辞書で検索しやすいように見出しをつけていますので、理解できるまで、自分で調べることが大切です。この「じっくりと読んで理解する」作業を怠ると、学習効果は半減します。粘り強く繰り返すことで、知らず知らずのうちに「読める」ようになるのです。

◆【段落要旨・百字要約】

　各段落ごとの要旨を完成させて、百字要約につなげる演習をします。この演習を繰り返すことで、国公立大の二次試験で問われる「要約力」「記述力」を効率的に養うことができます。

　やみくもに「書く」ことを繰り返しても、要約する力は身につきません。要約文を完成させるためには、「必要な情報と不必要な情報の選別」と「必要な情報をつなぎ合わせること」に慣れる必要があります。ここではその2点を意識しながら演習できるように構成されています。

● 目次 ●

The recipe for making any creature is written in its DNA. So last year, when geneticists★ published the near-complete DNA sequence of the long-extinct woolly mammoth, there was much speculation about whether we could bring this giant creature back to life.

Creating a living, breathing creature from a genome★ sequence that exists only in a computer's memory is not possible right now. But someone someday is sure to try it, predicts Stephan Schuster, a molecular biologist at Pennsylvania State University and a driving force behind the mammoth genome project.

So besides the mammoth, what other extinct beasts might we bring back to life? Well, 🕪 2 it is only going to be possible with creatures for which we can recover a complete genome sequence. (1)Without one, there is no chance. And usually when a creature dies, the DNA in any flesh left untouched is soon destroyed as it is attacked by sunshine and bacteria.

There are, however, some circumstances in which DNA can be preserved. If your specimen froze to death in an icy wasteland such as Siberia, or died in a dark cave or a really dry region, for instance, then the probability of finding some intact stretches of DNA is much higher.

Even in ideal conditions, though, no genetic information is likely to survive more 🕪 3 than a million years — so dinosaurs are out — and only much younger remains are likely to yield good-quality DNA. "It's really only worth studying specimens that are less than 100,000 years old," says Schuster.

The genomes of several extinct species besides the mammoth are already being sequenced, but (2)turning these into living creatures will not be easy. "It's hard to say that something will never ever be possible," says Svante Pääbo of the Max Planck Institute for Evolutionary Anthropology in Germany, "but it would require technologies so far removed from what we currently have that I cannot imagine how it would be done."

But then (3)50 years ago, who would have believed we would now be able to read the 🕪 4 instructions for making humans, fix inherited diseases, clone mammals and be close to creating artificial life? Assuming that we will develop the necessary technology, we have selected ten extinct creatures that might one day be resurrected. Our choice is based not just on practicality, but also on each animal's "charisma" — just how exciting the prospect of resurrecting these animals is.

Of course, bringing extinct creatures back to life raises a number of further problems, such as where they will live, but let's not (4).

＊ geneticist「遺伝学者」 genome「ゲノム（生物の生活機能を維持するための最小限の遺伝子群を含む染色体の一組）」

1 Without (A)(   ), there is no chance of
(B)(   ).

2 ・
・

3

4

5

6

7

語句	音声は、「英語」→「日本語の意味」の順で読まれます。	CD 1- Tr 5-8

入試基礎レベル

2 **publish** [pʌ́bliʃ] ....

9 **besides ...** ....

10 **recover** [rikʌ́vər] ....

22 **species** [spíːʃi(ː)z] ....

23 **turn A into B** ....

26 **currently** [kə́ːrəntli] ....

28 **instruction** [instrʌ́kʃən] ....

30 **not just A but also B** ....

33 **raise** [réiz] (動) ....

33 **a number of ...** ....

33 **further** [fə́ːrðər] (形) ....

34 **such as ...** ....

入試標準レベル（共通テスト・私大）

1 **creature** [kríːtʃər] ....

3 **bring ... back to life** ....

6 **be sure to** *do* ....

7 **predict** [pridíkt] ....

9 **extinct** [ekstíŋkt] ....

9 **beast** [bíːst] ....

12 **destroy** [distrɔ́i] ....

14 **circumstance** [sə́ːrkəmstæns] ....

14 **preserve** [prizə́ːrv] ....

15 **cave** [kéiv] ....

16 **region** [ríːdʒən] ....

16 **probability** [prὰbəbíləti] ....

18 **ideal** [aidíːəl] ....

18 **genetic information** 遺伝情報

20 **yield** [jíːld] (動) ....

20 **worth** *doing* ....

24 **never ever** ....

28 **fix** [fíks] (動) 治療する、回復させる

28 **mammal** [mǽməl] ....

28 **be close to** *doing* ....

29 **assume** [əsjúːm] ....

32 **prospect** [prάspekt] (名) ....

....

34 **spoil** [spɔ́il] (動) ....

入試発展レベル（二次・有名私大）

1 **recipe** [résəpi] ....

3 **speculation** [spèkjəléiʃən] ....

12 **flesh** [fléʃ] (名) ....

16 **a stretch of ...** ....

19 **remains** [riméinz] ....

30 **resurrect** [rèzərékt] ....

31 **practicality** [præktikǽləti] ....

その他

2 **near-complete** ほぼ完全な、完全に近い

2 **DNA sequence** DNA 配列

2 **long-extinct** 大昔に絶滅した

2 **woolly** [wúli] (形) 毛に覆われた、毛深い

2 **woolly mammoth** ケナガマンモス

7 **molecular biologist** 分子生物学者

8 **driving force behind ...**

.........................…を支える原動力

12 **untouched** [ʌntʌ́tʃt] 手つかずの、無傷の

13 **bacteria** [bæktíəriə] バクテリア、細菌

15 **specimen** [spésəmin] 標本、検査サンプル

15 **icy wasteland** [wéistlænd]

.........................氷に覆われた不毛の地

16 **intact** [intǽkt] 無傷の、完全な

19 **out** [áut] (形) 受け入れられない

23 **sequence** [síːkwəns] (動)

.........................並べる、配列を決定する

28 **inherited disease** 遺伝病、遺伝性疾患

28 **clone** [klóun] (動) （〜の）クローンを作る

31 **charisma** [kərízmə] カリスマ性

展開	段落	要旨
序論	1	（①　　　　　　　　　）のほぼ完全な（②　　　　　　）配列の発表は、その復活の可能性について多くの推測を呼んだ。
本論①	2	（③　　　　　）配列から生物を作ることは、現在不可能だ。
本論②	3	絶滅種の復活には完全な（③　　　　　）配列の復元が不可欠だが、生物の死後、（②　　　　　）は太陽光や（④　　　　　　）で急速に破壊される。
本論③	4	死体が低温や暗部、乾燥などの条件下で保存されると、無傷の（②　　　　　）が見つかる可能性が高い。
本論④	5	良質の（②　　　　　）抽出の可能性は経過年数の短い死体で高く、調査価値があるのは（⑤　　　　　）年未満の標本だけだ。
本論⑤	6	（③　　　　　）配列からの生物創造には、現在とは全く異なる技術が必要だ。
結論	7	科学者は将来の技術開発を想定し、復活の可能性がある絶滅種を（⑥　　　　　）種選定した。
結論の補強	8	絶滅種の復活は多くの問題を引き起こすだろうが、その楽しみを台無しにするのはやめておこう。

百字要約　「段落要旨」を参考にして、本文全体の内容を百字程度の日本語で要約しなさい。

（下書き）　　　　　　　　　　　　　　　　　10　　　　　　　　　　　　　　　　　20

本文解説

1 【besides】

(l.9) So **besides** the mammoth, what other extinct beasts might we bring back to life?

▶ besides は beside「〔前〕…のそばに」から派生した語だが、「〔前〕…の他に、…に加えて (in addition to ...)、〔副〕その上、さらに (in addition, furthermore)」の意味。ここは「マンモス以外に、他にどんな絶滅動物が…」。
  cf. I don't like the color of this sweater, and besides it's more than I can afford.
  「このセーターは色が気に入らないし、それに高くて買えないわ」

2 【leave O *done*】

(l.11) And usually when a creature dies, the DNA in any flesh **left untouched** is soon destroyed as it is attacked by sunshine and bacteria.

▶ 主節の主部は the DNA in any flesh left untouched まで。
▶ left untouched (= which is left untouched) は「無傷のままで残された」。is left untouched は leave ... untouched「…を手つかずのままにしておく」の受動態。
▶ この leave は「〜のままの状態にしておく」の意味で、〈leave + O + C〉の形で用いる。上記のように C に過去分詞形がくると「O が〜されたままにする」。
  ex. Several questions were left unanswered.「いくつかの質問は答えが出されないままだった」

3 【though】【out】【it is worth (while) *doing*】

(l.18) Even in ideal conditions, **though,** / no genetic information is likely to survive more than a million years — so dinosaurs are **out** — and only much younger remains are likely to yield good-quality DNA. "**It's** really only **worth studying** specimens that are less than 100,000 years old," says Schuster.

▶ この though は副詞で「しかし、けれども (= however)」。though の後にポーズを置いて読む。文中に置かれているが、前文とは異なる内容であることを示したり、前文の内容を弱めたりするので、日本語では「しかし (たとえ前段落で述べたような) 理想的な状態であっても、」となるだろう。文末にくることもある。
▶ この out は not possible or not allowed「不可能で、受け入れられない、問題外で」の意味。「遺伝情報が 100 万年を超えて存在し続ける可能性はほとんどない。だから (100 万年以上前に絶滅した〔参考：恐竜の大部分は約 6,550 万年前の白亜紀に絶滅したとされる〕) 恐竜は (DNA の抽出は) 無理だ」ということ。
  ex. His proposal is definitely out.「彼の提案は全く論外だ (受け入れられない)」
▶ it is worth (while) *doing* は「〜するのは (時間をかけるだけの) 価値がある」。it は形式主語で、真主語は *doing* である。worth については次のような使い方を覚えておこう。
  ex. It is worth (while) reading the book. = It is worth while to read the book.
    = The book is worth reading.「その本は一読の価値がある」

4 【assuming that ...】

(l.29) **Assuming that** we will develop the necessary technology, we have selected ten extinct creatures that might one day be resurrected.

▶ assuming that ... は、「仮に…だとすると」の意味で if ... と同意に使われる用法もあるが、ここは「…という仮定のもとに (= based on the assumption that ...)」と解釈できる。「必要な技術が将来開発されるだろうと想定して、我々はいつかよみがえらせることができるかもしれない絶滅動物を 10 種選んだ」。
  cf. Assuming that this information is correct, we must change our plan.
    「もしこの情報が正しいとすれば、我々は計画を変更しなければならない」

Memo

CD 1

⊚9

There is a dirty little secret known to health professionals that they do not usually much talk about. Let's assume that you follow the recommendations of a health authority and get out there most days to go jogging, even though you would much rather be doing something else. Say you get ready, warm up, jog, and cool down for about an hour a day, which is a modest regimen.

⊚10

Over a year, you will spend about 360 hours doing this, and during 40 years (say, from age twenty-one to age sixty-one), you will spend about (X) hours. Assuming that most of us are awake for about 16 hours a day, this means that you would be spending the equivalent of about (Y) days jogging. This is about two and a half years spent exercising.

⊚11

How much longer would such an active person live? How many extra days of life would this diligent jogger gain in which to pursue other well-loved hobbies? We do not know for sure, but anything that increased average (Z) by more than two and a half years in a generally healthy adult population would be considered a very large effect — a striking phenomenon. (1)So, with two and a half years spent on the pavement, there is not likely to be much of a net* gain in available time for our poor jogger. Anyone who exercised even more would gain even less, winding up with a net loss of time. But it gets even worse. Note that in this contrived example, the unhappy jogger is trading away thousands of hours of youth for perhaps a few extra years in old age. Many individuals would not choose (2)that trade-off. They would prefer to have their leisure time when they are young and healthy.

⊚12

Of course the real picture is somewhat more complicated. The jogger might really enjoy jogging and so might consider the time well spent. Or the jogger might be warding off a diagnosed tendency toward a debilitating chronic disease such as diabetes. (3)Still, for many reasonably healthy and active individuals who are out running every morning because some advice list or some friend is pressuring them to try to improve their health, the results are not necessarily going to be what they expect. Some might have better uses for all that time, and others will be harmed by running injuries or even sudden death from cardiac arrest.

⊚13

From a public health point of view, it's great that so many people these days like to engage in socially hyped challenges like marathons. (4)But it is important to recognize that these are recent social phenomena, and that many people in the past remained steadily active in a healthy way having never even heard of a jogging trail or a spinning class*.

* net「正味の」
spinning class「スピニングのクラス (spinning は米国を発祥の地とする、ジムなどで行うバイク・エクササイズ)」

1 (X) ＿＿＿＿＿＿＿＿＿＿＿＿＿＿＿ (Y) ＿＿＿＿＿＿＿＿＿＿＿＿＿＿＿

2 ....

3

									10										20

4 ....

5 ....

....

6 ....

....

7 ....

語句　音声は、「英語」→「日本語の意味」の順で読まれます。　　　CD 1- Tr 14-17

入試基礎レベル

1　(be) known to ...

12　gain [géin]（動）

13　for sure

16　available [əvéiləbl]

20　individual [ìndəvídʒuəl]（名）

20　prefer to *do*

28　harm [háːrm]（動）

28　injury [índʒəri]

入試標準レベル（共通テスト・私大）

2　assume [əsjúːm]

2　recommendation [rèkəməndéiʃən]

3　even though ...

3　would rather *do*

5　modest [mádəst]

9　equivalent of ...

12　pursue [pərsjúː]

15　striking [stráikiŋ]（形）

15　phenomenon [finámənàn]

22　somewhat [sʌ́mhwʌ̀t]

24　tendency toward ...

30　point of view

31　challenge [tʃǽlindʒ]（名）

33　steadily [stédəli]

33　hear of ...

入試発展レベル（二次・有名私大）

3　authority [əθɔ́ːrəti]

4　say ...

12　diligent [dílidʒənt]

15　pavement [péivmənt]

19　trade away ... for ～

20　trade-off

24　diagnose [dàiəgnóus]

24　chronic disease

26　pressure ... to *do*

語句　　音声は、「英語」→「日本語の意味」の順で読まれます。　　CD 1- Tr 14-17

その他

5	**regimen** [rédʒəmən]	運動療法、食事療法
13	**longevity** [lɑndʒévəti]	寿命、長生き
16	**net gain**	純益
17	**wind up with ...**	最終的に…になる
17	**net loss**	純損失
18	**contrived** [kəntráivd](形)	不自然な、うそっぽい
24	**ward off ...**	…を避ける、防ぐ

24	**debilitating** [dibílitèitiŋ](形)	衰弱性の
24	**diabetes** [dàiəbí:ti:z]	糖尿病
25	**reasonably** [rí:znəbli]	ほどほどに
29	**cardiac arrest**	心(拍)停止、心不全
30	**public health**	公衆衛生
31	**hype** [háip]	誇大に宣伝する
33	**jogging trail**	ジョギングコース

段落要旨　　各段落のまとめとなるように、空所に適切な語句を入れなさい。（同じ番号には、同じ語句が入ります）

展開	段落	要旨
主題の提示	1	健康法に関して、（①　　　　　　　）だけに知られているちょっとした秘密がある。
例示	2	1日1時間のジョギングは、40年間で約（②　　　　　　　）を運動に費やした計算になる。
主題の展開①	3	走る時間の合計と寿命の延びには大差がなく、老齢期の数年間の代わりに貴重な（③　　　　　　　）の時間を失っているとも言える。
主題の展開②	4	ジョギングをする理由はさまざまだが、多くの人にとっては、必ずしも期待通りの結果が出るとは限らず、（④　　　　　　　）や死の危険すらある。
主題の展開③	5	最近の走るという（⑤　　　　　　　）は、公衆衛生上は好ましいことだが、昔は多くの人が走らなくても健康だった。

百字要約　　「段落要旨」を参考にして、本文全体の内容を百字程度の日本語で要約しなさい。

（下書き）

1 【文構造】

(l.1) There is a dirty little secret known to health professionals **that they do not usually much talk about.**

> ▶ that 以下は関係代名詞節で、先行詞は a dirty little secret。known to health professionals も a dirty little secret を修飾しているので、全体は「医療従事者には知られているが、ふだん彼らがあまり話題にしない、ちょっとしたひどい秘密がある」。

2 【say の用法】

(l.4) **Say** you get ready, warm up, jog, and cool down for about an hour a day, which is a modest regimen.

(l.6) Over a year, you will spend about 360 hours doing this, and during 40 years (**say**, from age twenty-one to age sixty-one), you will spend about 14,400 hours.

> ▶ 第 1 文の Say ... は「…だと仮定する、もし…ならば」の意味で、Suppose ... と同意。
> *ex.* Say you had one million yen, what would you like to do with the money?
> 「仮にあなたが 100 万円持っていたとしたら、そのお金で何をしたいですか」
> ▶ 第 2 文の say は挿入句的に用いられて「例えば (= for example)」の意味。let's say と言うこともある。
> *ex.* Can you come here again tomorrow morning? Say, 9:30.
> 「明朝もう一度ここに来られますか？ 例えば、9 時半はどうですか」

3 【前置詞＋関係代名詞＋ to *do*】

(l.11) How many extra days of life would this diligent jogger gain **in which to pursue** other well-loved hobbies?

> ▶ in which to pursue other well-loved hobbies は、離れてはいるが extra days of life を説明している。〈前置詞＋関係代名詞＋ to *do*〉は文語的な用法で、ここは in which this diligent jogger would pursue other well-loved hobbies あるいは when this diligent jogger would pursue ... と書き換えることができる。全体で「この勤勉なジョガーは、他の大好きな趣味を追求する日を、一生の中で何日余分に獲得できるだろうか」。
> *ex.* Jamie is looking for a place in which to live.「ジェイミーは住居を探している」
> I have no words with which to express my gratitude.「(私の感謝の気持ちを表現するいかなる言葉も持たない→) 何とお礼を申し上げていいかわかりません」

4 【anything の用法】【仮定法】

(l.12) We do not know for sure, but **anything that increased** average longevity by more than two and a half years in a generally healthy adult population **would be considered** a very large effect — a striking phenomenon.

> ▶ 肯定文の anything は「どれでも、何でも」を意味するので、ここも anything that increased ... で「…を延ばすものはどんなものでも」。
> *ex.* "Which flavor do you want?" —"Any one of these will do, if it is not too sour."
> 「どの味にしますか」—「酸っぱすぎなければ、この中のどれでもいいですよ」
> ▶ increased, would be considered が仮定法であることに注意。主部の anything that increased ... population に「もし…を延ばすようなものがあるとすれば、それはどんなものでも」と仮定の意味が含まれていて、それを述部で would be considered a very large effect — a striking phenomenon「非常に大きな効果 — 際だった現象 — と見なされるであろう」と受けている。

5 【note の用法】【trade】

(l.18) **Note that** in this contrived example, the unhappy jogger is **trading away** thousands of hours of youth **for** perhaps a few extra years in old age.

> ▶ note that ... で「…ということに注目する、気をつける」。ここは命令形で「…に注目してみよう」の意味。
> ▶ trade away ... for ～「～と交換に…を引き渡す」 この for は〈交換・代償〉を表す用法で、for perhaps a few extra years in old age で「老齢期に追加されるかもしれないおよそ 2 ～ 3 年と交換に」。
> *ex.* Can I change this shirt for a larger size?「このシャツ、大きなサイズに交換できますか」

CD 1

This actually did happen to a real person, and the real person is me. I had gone to ◉18
catch a train. This was April 1976, in Cambridge, U.K. I was a bit early for the train.
I'd gotten the time of the train wrong. I went to get myself a newspaper to do the
crossword, and a cup of coffee and a packet of cookies. I went and sat at a table. I want
5 you to picture the scene. It's very important that you get this very clear in your mind.
Here's the table, newspaper, cup of coffee, packet of cookies. There's a guy sitting
opposite me, perfectly ordinary-looking guy wearing a business suit, carrying a briefcase.
It didn't look like he was going to do anything weird. What he did was this: he suddenly
leaned across, picked up the packet of cookies, tore it open, took one out, and ate it.

10   Now (1)this, I have to say, is the sort of thing the British are very bad at dealing with. ◉19
There's nothing in our background, upbringing, or education that teaches you how to
deal with someone who in broad daylight has just stolen your cookies. You know what
would happen if this had been South Central Los Angeles. There would have very
quickly been gunfire, helicopters coming in, CNN, you know ... But in the end, I did
15 what any red-blooded Englishman would do: [2]. And I stared at the newspaper,
took a sip of coffee, tried to do a clue in the newspaper, couldn't do anything, and
thought, *What am I going to do?*

      In the end I thought, *Nothing for it, I'll just have to go for it*, and I tried very hard not ◉20
to notice the fact that the packet was already mysteriously opened. I took out a cookie
20 for myself. I thought, *That settled him*. But (3)it hadn't because a moment or two later
he did it again. He took another cookie. Having not mentioned it the first time, it was
somehow even harder to raise the subject the second time around. "Excuse me, I
couldn't help but (4)notice ..." I mean, it doesn't really work.

      We went through the whole packet like this. When I say the whole packet, I mean ◉21
25 there were only about eight cookies, but it felt like a lifetime. He took one, I took one,
he took one, I took one. Finally, when we got to the end, he stood up and walked away.
Well, we exchanged meaningful looks, then he walked away, and I breathed a sigh of
relief and sat back.

      A moment or two later the train was coming in, so I tossed back the rest of my ◉22

coffee, stood up, picked up the newspaper, and underneath the newspaper were my
cookies. The thing I like particularly about this story is the sensation that somewhere in
England there has been wandering around for the last quarter-century a perfectly
ordinary guy who's had the same exact story, only he doesn't have (5)the punch line.

語句　音声は、「英語」→「日本語の意味」の順で読まれます。　CD 1- Tr 23-26

入試基礎レベル

7	**perfectly** [pə́ːrfik*t*li]	
11	**background** [bǽkgràund]	
12	**steal** [stíːl]	
15	**stare at ...**	
19	**notice** [nóutəs]（動）	
21	**mention** [ménʃən]（動）	
27	**exchange** [ikstʃéind*ʒ*]（動）	

入試標準レベル（共通テスト・私大）

4	**packet** [pǽkət]（名）	
5	**picture** [píktʃər]（動）	
6	**guy** [gái]	
7	**business suit**	
10	**the British**	
10	**be bad at ...**	
10	**deal with ...**	
16	**clue** [klúː]	
19	**mysteriously** [mistíəriəsli]	
20	**settle** [sétl]	
23	**can't help but** *do*	
23	**work** [wə́ːrk]（動）	
25	**lifetime** [láiftàim]	
29	**the rest**	
32	**wander around**	
32	**quarter-century**	

入試発展レベル（二次・有名私大）

7	**briefcase** [bríːfkèis]	
8	**weird** [wíərd]	
9	**lean across**	
9	**tear ... open**	
16	**take a sip of ...**	
18	**go for it**	
22	**the second time around**	
31	**sensation** [senséiʃən]	

その他

7	**ordinary-looking**（形）	普通に見える
11	**upbringing** [ʌ́pbrìŋiŋ]	教育、養育、しつけ
12	**in broad daylight**	白昼堂々と
14	**gunfire** [gʌ́nfàiər]	発砲、銃声
15	**red-blooded**	本物の、生粋の
24	**go through ...**	…を使い果たす、全部使う
27	**meaningful look**	意味ありげな目つき
27	**breathe a sigh of relief**	ほっとしてため息をつく
28	**sit back**	（いすに）深く座る
29	**toss back ...**	…を一気に飲み干す
31	**punch line**	（ジョークの）落ち

展開	段落	要旨
物語の導入	1	筆者が駅で（①　　　　　　　）、コーヒー、（②　　　　　　　　　）を買ってテーブルにつくと、向かいに座ったまったく普通に見える男が、突然筆者の（②　　　　　　　）の袋を破って1枚取り出して食べてしまった。
物語の展開①	2	（③　　　　　　　）が対処を不得手とするたぐいの出来事であったので筆者は動揺するが、結局それを無視することにした。しかし、その後「（④　　　　　　　　　　　　　　　）」と考えた。
物語の展開②	3	思い切って自分も（②　　　　　　）に手を伸ばし1枚食べると、男もまた1枚取り出して食べた。いまさら指摘するわけにもいかない状況であった。
物語の展開③	4	2人が（②　　　　　　）を1袋まるごと食べ終えると、意味ありげな視線を互いに交わした後、男は歩き去り、筆者は安堵した。
物語の展開④	5	（⑤　　　　　　　）が入ってきたので立ち上がり（①　　　　　　　）を持ち上げると、その下に自分の（②　　　　　　）の袋を見つけ、自分の誤りにようやく気づいた。

（下書き）

10　　　　　　　　　　　　　　　　　　20

10　　　　　　　　　　　　　　　　　　20

本文解説

1 【go for it】

(l.18) In the end I thought, *Nothing for it, I'll just have to* **go for it**, and I tried very hard not to notice the fact that the packet was already mysteriously opened. I took out a cookie for myself.

▶ Nothing for it = There's nothing else I can do for it「私がそれに対して他にできることはない」
▶ just have to *do*「〜するしかない」 *ex.* It can't be helped, so I guess I'll just have to grin and bear it.「それはどうしようもないことだから、笑って耐えるしかないだろう」
▶ go for it はイディオムで「いちかばちかやってみる、頑張ってやってみる」。この場面での具体的内容は続く部分からわかるように、「クッキーの袋が男によって開けられ食べられたという事実は無視して、自分のクッキーに手を伸ばして食べる」ことである。go for it = reach for it(=a cookie) in a decisive manner と解釈していいだろう。

2 【分詞構文の意味上の主語】

(l.21) **Having not mentioned** it the first time, **it** was somehow even harder to raise the subject the second time around.

▶ この文では分詞構文の主語は明示されていないので、原則からは主節の主語と同じ it となるはずだが、内容からは I（筆者）である。意味を汲んで書き直すと、Since I had not mentioned it the first time, it was somehow even harder to raise the subject the second time around. となる。
▶ 分詞構文の意味上の主語が主節の主語と異なる場合、その主語を表さなければならない。そうした分詞構文を独立分詞構文と呼ぶが、時折その主語も明示されない場合がある。文法的に誤りとされることが多いが、実際は上記の例のようによく見かける。
  ex. Walking in Central Park, it's hard to believe you're in the middle of a big city.
  「セントラルパークを散歩していると、大都会の真ん中にいるとは信じがたい」

3 【倒置】

(l.29) A moment or two later the train was coming in, so I tossed back the rest of my coffee, stood up, picked up the newspaper, and **underneath the newspaper were my cookies**.

▶ 場所を示す副詞句（underneath the newspaper）が先頭に置かれ、主語（my cookies）と動詞（were）の位置が逆になる「倒置」が使われている。本来の語順は my cookies were underneath the newspaper である。
▶ the newspaper という古い既知の情報を文頭に置き、新しい伝えたい情報 my cookies を最後に置くことで、強調する効果がある。

4 【文構造】

(l.31) (S)The thing I like particularly about this story (V)is (C)the sensation that somewhere in England there has been wandering around for the last quarter-century a perfectly ordinary guy who's had the same exact story, only he doesn't have the punch line.

▶ The thing I like particularly about this story が文全体の主部、is が述語動詞、the sensation 以下が補語である。the sensation that somewhere in England ... exact story の that は同格節を導く接続詞で、全体は「イングランドのどこかに…だという感覚」。
▶ somewhere 以下は、somewhere in England / **there has been wandering around** / for the last quarter-century / **a perfectly ordinary guy** / who's had the same exact story と区切って読む。文の基本部分は there has been wandering around a perfectly ordinary guy「まったく普通の男がずっと歩き回っている」で、事実上の主部は a perfectly ordinary guy である。
▶ there has been wandering ... the same exact story は、a perfectly ordinary guy who's had the same exact story has been wandering around for the last quarter-century としても、意味の上ではあまり違いはない。

Memo

The English language is full of words which have changed their meanings slightly or even dramatically over the centuries. Changes of meaning can be of a number of different types. Some words, such as *nice*, have changed gradually. Emotive words tend to change more rapidly by losing some of their force, so that *awful*, which originally 5 meant 'inspiring awe', now means 'very bad' or, in expressions such as *awfully good*, simply something like 'very'. In any case, all connection with 'awe' has been lost.

Some changes of meaning, though, seem to attract more attention than others. (1)This is perhaps particularly the case where the people who worry about such things believe that a distinction is being lost. For example, there is a lot of concern at the 10 moment about the words *uninterested* and *disinterested*. In modern English, the positive form *interested* has two different meanings. The first and older meaning is approximately 'having a personal involvement in', as in

　　He is an interested party in the dispute.

The second and later, but now much more common, meaning is 'demonstrating or 15 experiencing curiosity in, enthusiasm for, concern for,' as in

　　He is very interested in cricket.

(2)It is not a problem that this word has more than one meaning. Confusion never seems to occur, largely because the context will normally make it obvious which meaning is intended. In all human languages there are very many words which have more than 20 one meaning — this is a very common and entirely normal (3)state of affairs. Most English speakers, for example, can instantly think of a number of different meanings for the words *common* and *state* and *affairs* which I have just used.

Perhaps surprisingly, according to dictionaries the two different meanings of *interested* have different negative forms. The negative of the first meaning is *disinterested*, as in

25　　(4)*He is an interested party in the dispute, and I am disinterested and therefore able to be more objective about it.*

Disinterested is thus roughly equivalent to 'neutral, impartial'. The negative form of the second, more usual meaning is *uninterested*, as in

　　He is very interested in cricket, but I am uninterested in all sports.

Uninterested is thus roughly equivalent to 'bored, feeling no curiosity'.

⟿30   Now it happens that *interested*, in its original meaning, is today a rather unusual, learned, formal word in English. Most people, if they wanted to convey this concept in normal everyday speech, would probably say something like *not neutral*, or *biased* or *involved* or *concerned*. Recently, this unfamiliarity with the older meaning of the word (A) has led to many people now using (B) with the same meaning as (C):   35

  I am disinterested in cricket.

They have, perhaps, heard the word (D) and, not being aware of the meaning 'neutral, unbiased', they have started using it as the negative form of (E) in the more recent sense. Opponents of this change claim that this is an ignorant misuse of the word, and that a very useful distinction is being lost. What can we say about this?   40

解答欄

1
....
....
....

2
....
....

3
....

4
....
....

5 (A) .... (B) .... (C) .... (D) .... (E) ....

6
....

語句　音声は、「英語」→「日本語の意味」の順で読まれます。　CD 1 - Tr 31-34

入試基礎レベル

3　**gradually** [grǽdʒuəli]

3　**tend to** *do*

4　**force** [fɔ́ːrs]（名）

6　**something like ...**

6　**connection with ...**

20　**common** [kɑ́mən]

21　**think of ...**

25　**therefore** [ðéərfɔ̀ər]

30　**bored** [bɔ́ːrd]

32　**formal** [fɔ́ːrməl]

35　**lead to ...**

39　**claim** [kléim]（動）

入試標準レベル（共通テスト・私大）

2　**dramatically** [drəmǽtikəli]

4　**awful** [ɔ́ːfl]

4　**originally** [ərídʒənəli]

5　**awfully** [ɔ́ːfli]

6　**in any case**

9　**distinction** [distíŋkʃən]

9　**at the moment**

11　**approximately** [əprɑ́ksəmətli]

12　**involvement** [invɑ́lvmənt]

13　**dispute** [dispjúːt]（名）

14　**demonstrate** [démənstrèit]

15　**curiosity in ...**

15　**enthusiasm for ...**

15　**concern for ...**

17　**confusion** [kənfjúːʒən]

18　**context** [kɑ́ntekst]

18　**normally** [nɔ́ːrməli]

18　**obvious** [ɑ́bviəs]

19　**intend** [inténd]

20　**entirely** [entáiərli]

21　**instantly** [ínstəntli]

23　**surprisingly** [sərpráiziŋli]

26　**objective** [əbdʒéktiv]（形）

27　**thus** [ðʌ́s]

27　**roughly** [rʌ́fli]

27　**(be) equivalent to ...**

27　**neutral** [njúːtrəl]（形）

32　**learned** [lə́ːrnid]（形）　教養［学識］のある

32　**convey** [kənvéi]

32　**concept** [kɑ́nsept]（名）

34　**involved** [invɑ́lvd]

34　**concerned** [kənsə́ːrnd]

37　**(be) aware of ...**

39　**opponent** [əpóunənt]（名）

39　**ignorant** [ígnərənt]

入試発展レベル（二次・有名私大）

3　**emotive** [imóutiv]

10　**uninterested** [ʌníntərèstid]

10　**disinterested** [disíntərèstid]

13　**party** [pɑ́ːrti]（名）

20　**state of affairs**

27　**impartial** [impɑ́ːrʃəl]

33　**biased** [báiəst]

その他

5　**inspire awe**　畏敬の念を呼び起こす

33　**everyday speech**　日常言葉、日常会話

34　**unfamiliarity** [ʌnfəmiliǽrəti]　なじみがないこと

38　**unbiased** [ʌnbáiəst]　公平な、先入観のない

39　**misuse** [mìsjúːs]（名）　誤用

展開	段落	要旨
序論	1	英語には（①　　　　）が変化してきた単語が数多くある。
本論①	2	しかし、（①　　　　）の（②　　　　）が失われつつある場合、それは他の変化以上に注目を集める。現在、uninterested と disinterested についての懸念がある。肯定形である（③　　　　）には、異なる2つの（①　　　　）があるが、それが問題なのではない。
本論②	3	（③　　　　）の2つの異なる（①　　　　）には、それぞれ disinterested と uninterested という否定形がある。
本論③	4	今では、（③　　　　）の古い（①　　　　）はなじみがないものなので、多くの人がdisinterested と uninterested を同じ（①　　　　）で使う傾向にある。こうした変化について、それは（④　　　　）であって、有用な（②　　　　）が失われつつある、と反対する人たちもいる。

百字要約　「段落要旨」を参考にして、本文全体の内容を百字程度の日本語で要約しなさい。

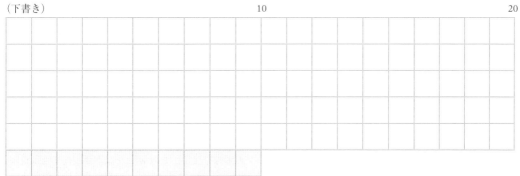

（下書き）

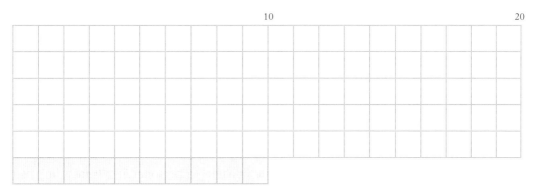

本文解説

1 【of の用法】【nice の意味の変遷】

(l.2) Changes of meaning can be **of a number of different types**. Some words, such as **nice**, have changed gradually.

- ▶ 〈of ＋名詞〉で「…のある、…の性質を持つ」の意味を表すものがある。ここは全体で「意味の変化にはいくつかの異なるタイプがありうる」の意味。
- ▶ history of the word *nice*: Derived from the Latin adjective *nescius* meaning "ignorant", the English word nice was borrowed in the 14th century from French as a term for "foolish" or "silly". It then changed its meaning gradually and took on the more neutral attributes of "shyness" or "reserve". The society in the 18th century admired such qualities, which brought on the more positively charged meanings of "nice" we know today.

2 【文構造】

(l.3) (S)Emotive words (V)tend to change more rapidly by losing some of their force, so that (S2)awful, which originally meant 'inspiring awe', now (V2)means (O2)'very bad' or, in expressions such as *awfully good*, (O3)simply something like 'very'.

- ▶ tend to *do*「～する傾向がある、～しがちである」 by losing some of their force で「その言葉が持つ強さをいくらか失うことによって」。by は〈手段・方法〉を表す用法。
- ▶ so that 以下の基本は so that *awful* now means 'very bad' or simply something like 'very' である。
- ▶ so that ～は結果を表現し「その結果～だ」。which originally meant 'inspiring awe' は非制限用法の関係詞節で、awful は「元々は『畏敬の念を引き起こす』という意味だったのだが」と説明している。in expressions such as *awfully good* は simply something like 'very' の実例を提示していて、「awfully good のような表現の中に見られるように」。something like ...「…のようなもの、およそ…」

3 【the case where ...】【文構造】

(l.8) This is perhaps particularly **the case where** (S')the people who worry about such things (V')believe (O')that a distinction is being lost.

- ▶ This は前文の「意味の変化の中には他の変化以上に注目を集めるものもある」という内容を指す。
- ▶ This is particularly the case where ... で「これは…の場合に特に当てはまる［言えることだ］。この case は通例 the をつけて「実情、事実 (fact)」の意味で、This is the case with ... の形で使うことが多く、「これは…の実情だ、これは…に関して当てはまる」の意味を表す。この where は関係副詞または接続詞と考えられるが、いずれにせよここでは接続詞的な用法で、「…の場合には、…のときには」の意味で使われている。この文を This is perhaps particularly true when ... と表現しても意味は変わらない。
- ▶ where 以下の主部は the people who worry about such things、述語動詞は believe、that 以下が目的語節。is being lost は進行形の受動態で、「失われつつある」。distinction「区別、差異」

【参考】文中の such things が指す内容はあいまい。入試問題で割愛されている先行段落中の "A number of people seem to think that the fact that languages change the meanings of their words in this way is unfortunate. They believe <u>that change in language is inherently undesirable and that we should do everything we can to stop it because change can be dangerous and confusing.</u>" の下線部分の内容を受けているものと思われる。

4 【as の用法】

(l.11) The first and older meaning is approximately 'having a personal involvement in', **as** in *He is an interested party in the dispute.*

- ▶ この as in ... は「（例えば）…において見られるような、…の場合のように」の意味で、この例のように例や例文を挙げるのに便利な用法。
- *ex.* "Did you say E or D?" "It's E. E as in elephant."「E って言ったの？それとも D ？」「E、エレファントの E です」（電話などでアルファベットの確認を行うときに使用される言い方）

Memo

When Mike May was three years old, a chemical explosion rendered him completely ⚙35 blind. This did not stop him from becoming the best blind downhill speed skier in the world, as well as a businessman and family man. Then, forty-three years after the explosion robbed him of his vision, he heard about a new surgical development that might be able to restore it. Although he was successful in his life as a blind man, he decided to undergo the surgery.

After the operation, the bandages were removed from around his eyes. Accompanied ⚙36 by a photographer, Mike sat on a chair while his two children were brought in. This was a big moment. It would be the first time he would ever gaze into their faces with his newly cleared eyes. In the resulting photograph, Mike has a pleasant but awkward smile on his face as his children smile at him.

(1)The scene was supposed to be touching, but it wasn't. There was a problem. ⚙37 Mike's eyes were now working perfectly, but he stared with utter puzzlement at the objects in front of him. His brain didn't know what to make of the overwhelming flow of information. He wasn't experiencing his sons' faces; he was experiencing only uninterpretable sensations of edges and colors and lights. Although his eyes were functioning, he didn't have vision.

And this is because the brain has to learn how to see. The strange electrical storms ⚙38 inside the pitch-black skull get turned into conscious summaries after a sustained effort of figuring out how objects in the world match up across the senses. Consider the experience of walking down a hallway. Mike knew from a lifetime of moving down corridors that walls remain parallel, at arm's length, the whole way down. So when his vision was restored, the concept of perspective lines meeting at a distant point was beyond his capacity to understand. (2)It made no sense to his brain.

Similarly, when I was a child I met a blind woman and was amazed at how intimately ⚙39 she knew the layout of her rooms and furniture. I asked her if she would be able to draw the layouts with higher accuracy than most sighted people. Her response surprised me: she said she would not be able to draw the layouts at all, because she didn't understand how sighted people converted three dimensions (the room) into two dimensions (a flat piece of paper). (3)The idea simply didn't make sense to her.

Vision does not simply exist when a person confronts the world with clear eyes. ⚙40

Instead, an interpretation of the electro-chemical signals streaming from the eyes to the brain has to be trained up. Mike's brain didn't understand how his own movements affected the way he saw objects. For example, when he moves his head to the left, the scene shifts to the right. The brains of sighted people have come to expect such things   35
and know how to ignore them. But Mike's brain was confused by these strange relationships. And this illustrates a key point: the conscious experience of vision occurs only when there is accurate prediction of sensory consequences. (4)So although vision seems like a representation of something that's objectively out there, it doesn't come for free. It has to be learned.   40

41   After moving around for several weeks, staring at things, kicking chairs, examining silverware, rubbing his wife's face, Mike came to have the experience of sight as we experience it. He now experiences vision the same way you do. He just appreciates it more.

1 (ア) ....

....

(イ) ....

....

....

2 (ア) ....

....

(イ) ....

....

3 ....

4 ....

....

5 ....

語句　音声は、「英語」→「日本語の意味」の順で読まれます。　CD 1- Tr 42-45

入試基礎レベル

1	completely [kəmplí:tli]
7	remove [rimú:v]
10	pleasant [pléznt]
13	stare at ...
14	flow [flóu] (名)
17	function [fʌ́ŋkʃən] (動)
18	electrical [iléktrikəl]
19	conscious [kánʃəs]
20	figure out ...
20	sense [séns] (名)
25	similarly [símələrli]
27	response [rispáns]
34	affect [əfékt]
36	confuse [kənfjú:z]
37	occur [əkə́:r]
43	appreciate [əprí:ʃièit]

入試標準レベル（共通テスト・私大）

2	blind [bláind] (形)
4	rob ... of ~
4	vision [víʒən]
5	restore [ristó:r]
7	operation [à(:)pəréiʃən]
7	accompany [əkʌ́mpəni]
10	clear [klíər] (動)
10	awkward [ɔ́:kwərd]
12	touching [tʌ́tʃiŋ] (形)
16	edge [édʒ] (名)
19	summary [sʌ́məri] (名)
21	hallway [hó:lwèi]
22	corridor [kó:rədər]
23	concept [kánsept] (名)
25	be amazed at ...
26	layout [léiàut]
26	furniture [fə́:rnitʃər]
29	convert ... into ~
29	dimension [dəménʃən]
31	confront [kənfrʌ́nt]
32	interpretation [intə̀:rpritéiʃən]
35	shift [ʃíft] (動)
36	ignore [ignó:r]
37	illustrate [íləstrèit]
38	accurate [ǽkjərət]

38	prediction [pridíkʃən]
38	consequence [kánsəkwèns]
39	representation [rèprizentéiʃən]
42	rub [rʌ́b] (動)

入試発展レベル（二次・有名私大）

1	render A B
4	surgical [sə́:rdʒikəl]
6	undergo surgery
7	bandage [bǽndidʒ]
9	gaze into ...
13	utter [ʌ́tər] (形)
13	puzzlement [pʌ́zəlmənt]
14	overwhelming [òuvərwélmiŋ] (形)
19	skull [skʌ́l]
22	parallel [pǽrəlèl] (形)
24	make no sense to ...
25	intimately [íntəmətli]
27	with accuracy
32	stream [strí:m] (動)
38	sensory [sénsəri]
39	objectively [əbdʒéktivli]

その他

2	downhill skier	滑降のスキーヤー
14	make ... of ~	～を…だと思う、理解する
16	uninterpretable [ʌ̀nintə́:rprətbl]	説明できない
19	pitch-black	真っ暗な
19	sustained effort	持続的な努力
20	match up	適合する、組み合わさる
21	lifetime of ...	生涯にわたる…
22	at arm's length	腕を伸ばしたところに
22	the whole way down	終わりまでずっと
23	perspective [pərspéktiv]	遠近法の
27	sighted [sáitid]	目の見える
32	electro-chemical	電気化学的な
33	train up ...	…を訓練する、育てる
37	key point	重要な点
42	silverware [sílvəwèə]	銀製食器

展開	段落	要旨
序論①	1	マイクは 46 歳のときに、視力回復の（①　　　　　）を受けることに決めた。
序論②	2	（①　　　　　）後、マイクは自分の 2 人の子どもたちと一緒に写真を撮った。
本論①	3	（①　　　　　）後、目は完全に機能していたが、マイクの（②　　　　）は情報の流れを理解することができず、マイクには（③　　　　　）がなかった。
本論②	4	（②　　　　）は見方を学ぶ必要があり、世の中の物体が様々な（④　　　　）とどう組み合わさるかを理解するために、持続的な努力を経なければならない。
本論③	5	自分の部屋の配置を詳細に知っている（③　　　　）障害の女性は、その（⑤　　　　　）を書けないだろうと言った。それは、3 次元から 2 次元への（⑥　　　　）方法がわからないからだ。
本論④	6	（③　　　　）は、見える目だけでは存在せず、目から（②　　　　）への電気化学的（⑦　　　　）の解釈が訓練される必要がある。（③　　　　　）は習得されるものなのだ。
本論⑤	7	マイクは数週間の試行錯誤を経て、私たちと同じ（③　　　　　）を経験するようになった。

（下書き）　　　　　　　　　　　　　　　　　　　10　　　　　　　　　　　　　　　　　　　20

（空欄の原稿用紙マス）

10　　　　　　　　　　　　　　　　　　　20

（空欄の原稿用紙マス）

本文解説

1 【話法】

(l.8) This was a big moment. It **would** be the first time he **would** ever gaze into their faces with his newly cleared eyes.

▶ This は「マイクが子どもたちの顔を自分の目で初めて見る瞬間」を指す。この過去の時点から見た未来（＝これから起こること）を "It would be the first time he would ever ..." と表現している。直接話法では "It will be the first time he will ever ..." となるが、地の文が過去形で書かれているので would になっている。直接話法、間接話法のいずれでもない中間的な形で、「描出話法」「中間話法」などと呼ばれる。

▶ the first time のあとに関係詞 when（あるいは that）が省略されている。

2 【make ... of ～】

(l.14) His brain didn't know **what to make of** the overwhelming flow of information.

▶ what to make of ... = what it(=his brain) should make of ...

▶ make ... of ～には次の2つの意味がある。ここでは②の意味。
① 「～で…を作る」 *ex.* What is this desk made of?「この机は何でできていますか」
② 「～を…だと思う、理解する」（what や anything を目的語とした否定文、疑問文で使われることが多い）
ex. What do you make of their offer?「彼らの提案をどう思いますか」

3 【get ＋過去分詞】【文構造】

(l.18) The strange electrical storms inside the pitch-black skull **get turned** into conscious summaries **after a sustained effort of figuring out how objects in the world match up across the senses**.

▶ 〈get ＋過去分詞〉は動作の受動態を表し、「…される」の意味。get turned into conscious summaries「意識的な要約へと変えられる」とは「要約されて意識に上る」ということ。
ex. Our dog got hit by a car last week. 「先週、うちの犬が車にはねられた」

▶ how objects in the world match up across the senses「世の中の物体が様々な感覚（＝五感）とどう組み合わさるか」が figuring out の目的語になっている。after a sustained effort of ...「…という持続的な努力のあとで」 figure out ...「…を理解する、解明する」 match up「適合する、組み合わさる」

4 【同格の of】【動名詞の意味上の主語】

(l.22) So when his vision was restored, **the concept of perspective lines meeting at a distant point** was beyond his capacity to understand.

▶ the concept of ... の of は「同格」の用法で、「…という概念」の意味。perspective lines は動名詞 meeting の意味上の主語になっていて、全体で「遠近法の線が遠くの点で交わるという概念」。

▶ beyond *one's* capacity to *do*「…が～できる能力を越えて、…が～できないほどの」

5 【the way S ＋ V ...】

(l.43) He now experiences vision **the same way you do**.

▶ 〈the way S ＋ V ...〉の the way は接続詞的な用法で、「S が…するように」。the same way you do「あなたがたがそうする（＝ experience vision）のと同様に」。in the same way you do あるいは just as you do とも表現できる。
ex. I want to be able to speak English the way our teacher does.
「私は私たちの先生のように英語が話せるようになりたい」

Memo

CD 1
46

Climate change isn't new. Our planet is always changing and its environment rarely stays still for long. There have been times in the distant past when levels of CO_2 were much higher than they are today, and Antarctica, a continent around the South Pole, was a tropical paradise. There have been others when CO_2 levels were much lower, and there was even ice in what are now tropical areas. But over the past ten thousand years the Earth's climate has been unusually steady. We humans have become used to a world where the temperature hasn't changed much. In other words, we have been lucky. Now our steady reliable climate is changing, and this time nature isn't to blame. But how do we know for certain that the world is warming?

47

When you're trying to determine whether the world's temperature is rising, the biggest problem is picking out a signal from the "background noise." Even in our relatively stable times, temperatures move up and down from one day to another, from season to season, from year to year, and from place to place. To be sure that (1)the trend is occurring, you need to take precise measurements from many different places around the world, and do so for an extremely long time. The world's longest survey is (2)the Central England Temperature Record, which is a result of the serious data-collecting habits of seventeenth-century British natural scientists. It covers a large region of England and stretches back to 1659. The impressive record shows clear signs of warming, especially toward the end of the twentieth century.

48

However, the record covers only a tiny part of the globe. Changes in England don't necessarily reflect changes in the United States or Brazil. It also doesn't go back far enough to reveal just how unusual our recent warm temperatures really are. How do they compare, for instance, to the apparent warm period in medieval times when grapes were grown in northern England? Or to the so-called Little Ice Age several hundred years ago, when the River Thames in London froze over completely so that people could gather and sell things on its solid surface? To answer these questions, scientists have come up with clever ways to expand the records geographically and extend them backward in time. These records are written not by humans, but by nature.

49

Every year, the average tree grows a ring of new wood around its trunk. In a good year the ring will be thicker, in a bad year, thinner. Researchers drill a small core into the side of the tree, about the size of a wine cork, take out the wood, and then count and measure. By examining trees that are different ages, (3)they have been able to create a temperature record extending more than a thousand years and from regions across northern Europe, Russia, and North America.

50   In the frozen north and south, ice also contains a record book of past climate. Each year's snowfall buries the previous one. If temperatures are cold enough, the snow stays around long enough to be squeezed into ice, clearly marking out the annual layers because summer's snow crystals are larger than winter's, or because more dust blows in each year with the winter winds. (4)<u>The amount of snow that fell</u>   40
<u>in a given year gives clues as to how warm it was then.</u>

51   By fitting together a variety of measures like these, researchers have come to remarkably similar conclusions about temperatures over the last thousand years. The eleventh century was indeed relatively warm, corresponding to the Medieval Warm Period. Temperatures were cooler in the seventeenth century, corresponding to the   45
Little Ice Age, and again in the early nineteenth century. These warm and cool periods apparently were also fairly widespread.

52   However, it was only in the twentieth century that temperatures really began to rise noticeably. The warming didn't happen regularly, but in two bursts — which turns out to be important. The first one occurred during the early years of the   50
century and was marked enough that it made itself clearly felt. The second burst of warming began in the 1970s and has been gathering pace ever since. And, crucially, the temperatures we are experiencing now are hotter than they have been for the entire last thousand years. Even the Medieval Warm Period was cooler than it is today.   55

53   Let's look at some numbers. On a global scale, from the 1910s to the 1940s, average temperatures rose by about 0.3°C. After that there was a cooling of about 0.1°C, and since 1970 the world has warmed by a further 0.6°C. These numbers might not sound like much, but they are very significant. (5)<u>Although the temperature</u>
<u>where you live can change by much more than this within the space of a few hours</u>   60
<u>or days, it is much more worrying when global annual averages show a clear upward</u>
<u>trend.</u> Averaging in this way smooths out short-term differences and shows what's really happening. That's why a small change in global average temperature can reflect a very big shift in climate. Speaking in global averages, only a few degrees separate us from the frozen world of the last ice age.   65

1 ....

2 ....

3 ・

....

....

　　　・

....

....

4 ....

5 ....

....

6 ....

7 ....

....

....

8 ....

<table>

	入試基礎レベル	
18	impressive [imprésiv]	
23	apparent [əpǽrənt]	
26	gather [gǽðər]	
26	surface [sə́:rfəs]	
27	come up with ...	
33	measure [méʒər]（動）	
36	contain [kəntéin]	
42	measure [méʒər]（名）	
47	apparently [əpǽrəntli]	
64	degree [digrí:]	

</table>

	入試標準レベル（共通テスト・私大）	
6	steady [stédi]	
8	reliable [riláiəbl]	
9	for certain	
10	determine [ditə́:rmin]	
11	pick out A from B	
12	stable [stéibl]	
12	from one day to another	
14	precise [prisáis]	
15	extremely [ikstrí:mli]	
16	survey [sə́rvei]（名）	
17	cover [kʌ́vər]（動）	
18	region [rí:dʒən]	
22	reveal [riví:l]	
23	medieval [mì:díí:vəl]	
24	so-called [sóukɔ́:ld]	
26	solid [sάləd]	
28	geographically [dʒì:əgrǽfikli]	
28	extend [iksténd]	
37	bury [béri]	
37	previous [prí:viəs]	
41	clue [klú:]	
41	as to ...	
42	come to a conclusion	
43	remarkably [rimά:rkəbli]	
44	correspond to ...	
47	widespread [wáidspréd]	
49	burst [bə́:rst]（名）	
59	significant [signífikənt]	
61	worrying [wə́:riiŋ]（形）	

61	annual average	
62	average [ǽvəridʒ]（動）	
64	shift [ʃíft]（名）	
64	separate A from B	

	入試発展レベル（二次・有名私大）	
3	Antarctica [æntά:rktikə]	
3	the South Pole	
9	be to blame	
14	measurement [méʒərmənt]	
18	stretch back to ...	
30	trunk [trʌ́ŋk]（名）	
31	drill [dríl]（動）	
32	cork [kɔ́:rk]	
37	snowfall [snóufɔ̀:l]	
38	squeeze [skwí:z]	
38	mark out ...	
40	blow in	
41	given [gívn]（形）	
47	fairly [féərli]	
49	noticeably [nóutəsəbli]	
51	marked [mά:rkt]（形）	
52	crucially [krú:ʃli]	
62	smooth out	

	その他	
24	Little Ice Age	小氷河期
25	the River Thames	テムズ川
25	freeze over	氷結する、凍結する
28	backward in time	時間を遡って
30	ring [ríŋ]	（木の）年輪
32	core [kɔ́:r]	芯；円筒型標本、コア
38	stay around	存続し続ける、とどまる
39	annual layer	年層
39	snow crystal	雪の結晶
40	dust [dʌ́st]	ちり、ほこり
52	gather pace	ペースを速める
57	cooling [kú:liŋ]（名）	温度低下、冷却
60	within the space of ...	…（の期間）以内に
61	upward trend	上昇傾向

段落要旨 各段落のまとめとなるように、空所に適切な語句を入れなさい。（同じ番号には、同じ語句が入ります）

展開	段落	要旨
主題の 提示	1	（①　　　　　　　　）は目新しいものではないが、過去1万年間、地球の気候は驚くほど安定していた。今、地球は（②　　　　　　　）傾向にあるが、どうすればそれを確実に知ることができるか。
主題の 展開①	2	（②　　　　　　）傾向を判定するには、「バックグラウンドノイズ」から（①　　　　　　　）の（③　　　　　　　）を見つけ出さなければならず、多地域かつ長期間の正確な測定値が必要だ。
主題の 展開②	3	世界最長の記録でも不十分だ。科学者たちは、記録を地理的にも期間的にも拡大するため、（④　　　　　　　）の中に残された記録を利用する方法を考えた。
主題の 展開③	4	研究者たちは、異なる地域、異なる樹齢の木の（⑤　　　　　　）を測定し、（⑥　　　　　　　）年以上にわたる気温の記録を作成した。
主題の 展開④	5	（⑦　　　　　　）にも過去の気候が記されている。（⑦　　　　　　）の年層からわかる各年の雪の量が、その年の気候の手がかりとなる。
主題の 展開⑤	6	（④　　　　　　　）に残された記録によって、研究者たちは、過去（⑥　　　　　　　）年にわたる気温について似通った結論に達した。
主題の 展開⑥	7	（⑧　　　　　　）世紀だけに顕著な気温の上昇があり、1970年代以降はそのペースを速めている。そして現在の気温は、過去（⑥　　　　　　　）年間で最も高い。
結論	8	1970年以降、地球の平均気温は（⑨　　　　　　　）℃上昇したが、その数字の意味は大きい。平均気温の小さな変化が、気候の大きな変化を示すからだ。最後の氷河期と現在の平均気温の差は、わずか数度でしかない。

百字要約 「段落要旨」を参考にして、本文全体の内容を百字程度の日本語で要約しなさい。

（下書き）

									10										20

									10										20

1 【what の用法】

(l.4) There have been others when CO$_2$ levels were much lower, and there was even ice in **what** are now tropical areas.

> ▶ what are now tropical areas は「現在は熱帯地域である場所、現在の熱帯地域」の意味。関係代名詞 what は先行詞を含み「〜する物［事］、〜である物」を意味するが、thing(s) の意味範囲は幅広い。

2 【enough の用法】【make *oneself done*】

(l.21) It also doesn't go back far **enough to reveal** just how unusual our recent warm temperatures really are.

(l.50) The first one occurred during the early years of the century and was marked **enough** that **it made itself** clearly **felt**.

> ▶ 〈enough (for A) to *do*〉で「(A が) 〜するのに十分に」。第 1 文の It doesn't go back far enough to reveal 〜 は「それは〜を明らかにできるほど十分に過去に遡ってはいない」の意味。
> ▶ 第 2 文の〈enough (so) that A *do*〉は「A が〜するのに十分に」の意味を表す〈(主に) 米用法〉で、この例のように so が省かれることも多い。〈enough to *do*〉を使った (the first burst) was marked enough to make itself clearly felt と同意。
> ▶ it made itself felt は、He couldn't make himself understood in English.「彼は英語で意思を伝えられなかった」や She had to shout to make herself heard above the noise.「彼女は騒音にかき消されないように大声で叫ばなければならなかった」と同じ、〈make *oneself done*〉の形。〈make *oneself* felt〉は「自分 (の力) を印象づける、顕著な影響力を及ぼす」といった意味。it (= the first burst) was marked enough that it made itself clearly felt 全体で、「最初の爆発はそのことが明白に感じられるほど際立ったものだった」。

3 【compare の用法】【文構造】【関係副詞 when】【so that 〜 の用法】

(l.23) How do they **compare**, for instance, **to** the apparent warm period in medieval times when grapes were grown in northern England? Or **to** the so-called Little Ice Age several hundred years ago**, when** the River Thames in London froze over completely **so that** people could gather and sell things on its solid surface?

> ▶ 第 1 文の compare は自動詞用法。How does A compare to[with] B? で「A は B と比較してどうであるか？」。they は前文の our recent warm temperatures を指すので、「我々が経験している最近の暖かい気温は〜と比較して、どんな違い (あるいは類似点) があるのだろうか？」という意味。
> ▶ 第 2 文は第 1 文の続きで、or の直後に第 1 文冒頭の how do they compare を補って読む。
> ▶ , when ... の when は、直前の the so-called Little Ice Age several hundred years ago「数百年前のいわゆる小氷河期」を説明する、非制限用法の関係副詞。〈so that 〜〉は「結果」を表し、「(ロンドンのテムズ川が完全に氷結し) その結果人々は〜だった」の意味。

4 【文修飾の副詞】

(l.46) These warm and cool periods **apparently** were also fairly widespread.

(l.52) And, **crucially**, the temperatures we are experiencing now are hotter than they have been for the entire last thousand years.

> ▶ 上記の文の apparently, crucially は〈文修飾の副詞〉として働いている。第 1 文は It appears that these warm and cool periods were also fairly widespread. と書き換え可能で、「これらの温暖期と寒冷期はまた、かなり広範囲に及んでいたように思われる」の意味。It is apparent that ... とすると「…は明らかだ」という異なる意味になる。
> ▶ 第 2 文は It is crucial that [What is crucial is that] the temperatures we are experiencing now are hotter than they have been for the entire last thousand years. と書き換え可能で、「そして重要なことは、現在我々が経験している気温は、過去 1,000 年間全体 (のどの時期) よりも高いのだ」の意味。
> ▶ 〈文修飾の副詞〉には、文全体の内容に対する話し手の評価・判断を表すもの (apparently, possibly, probably, surely など) と、話し手の驚き・期待・当然などの反応を表す副詞 (fortunately, happily, surprisingly など) がある。置かれる位置は文頭が多いが、文中、文尾のこともある。

(1)<u>We are, to a remarkable degree, the right distance from the right sort of star</u>, one that is big enough to radiate lots of energy, but not so big as to burn itself out swiftly. It is a curiosity of physics that the larger a star the more rapidly it burns. Had our sun been ten times as massive, it would have exhausted itself after ten million years instead
5 of ten billion and we wouldn't be here now. We are also fortunate to orbit where we do. Too much nearer and everything on Earth would have boiled away. Much farther away and everything would have frozen.

In 1978, an astrophysicist named Michael Hart made some calculations and concluded that Earth would have been uninhabitable had it been just 1 percent farther
10 from or 5 percent closer to the Sun. (2)<u>That's not much, and in fact it wasn't enough.</u> The figures have since been refined and made a little more generous — 5 percent nearer and 15 percent farther are thought to be more accurate assessments for our zone of habitability — but that is still a narrow belt.

To appreciate just how narrow, you have only to look at Venus. Venus is only
15 twenty-five million miles closer to the Sun than we are. The Sun's warmth reaches it just two minutes before it touches us. In size and composition, Venus is very like Earth, but the small difference in orbital distance made all the difference to (3)<u>how it turned out.</u> It appears that during the early years of the solar system Venus was only slightly warmer than Earth and probably had oceans. But those few degrees of extra
20 warmth meant that Venus could not hold on to its surface water, with disastrous consequences for its climate. As its water evaporated, the hydrogen atoms escaped into space, and the oxygen atoms combined with carbon to form a dense atmosphere of the greenhouse gas CO_2. Venus became stifling. Although people of my age will recall a time when astronomers hoped that Venus might harbor life beneath its padded
25 clouds, possibly even a kind of tropical vegetation, we now know that it is much too fierce an environment for any kind of life that we can reasonably conceive of. Its surface temperature is a roasting 470 degrees centigrade (roughly 900 degrees Fahrenheit), which is hot enough to melt lead, and the atmospheric pressure at the surface is ninety times that of Earth, or more than any human body could withstand.
30 We lack the technology to make suits or even spaceships that would allow us to visit. Our knowledge of Venus's surface is based on distant radar imagery and some

disturbing noise from an unmanned Soviet probe that was dropped hopefully into the clouds in 1972 and functioned for barely an hour before permanently shutting down.

61   So that's what happens when you move two light minutes closer to the Sun. Travel farther out and the problem becomes not heat but cold, as Mars frigidly proves. It, 35 too, was once a much more congenial place, but couldn't retain a usable atmosphere and turned into a frozen waste.

1 the right distance: ....

....

the right sort of star: ....

....

2 ....

....

....

3 水 ： ....

CO_2 ： ....

温度 ： ....

気圧 ： ....

4

									10										20

5 ....

語句　音声は、「英語」→「日本語の意味」の順で読まれます。　CD 1 - Tr 62-65

入試基礎レベル

14 **appreciate** [əprí:ʃièit]

19 **slightly** [sláitli]

33 **function** [fʌ́ŋkʃən]（動）

35 **Mars** [má:rz]

入試標準レベル（共通テスト・私大）

1 **to a remarkable degree**

3 **curiosity** [kjùəriásəti]

3 **physics** [fíziks]

4 **massive** [mǽsiv]

7 **freeze** [frí:z]（動）

8 **calculation** [kæ̀lkjəléiʃən]

11 **generous** [dʒénərəs]

12 **accurate** [ǽkjərət]

16 **composition** [kàmpəzíʃən]

18 **the solar system**

21 **consequence** [kánsəkwèns]

22 **combine with ...**

22 **carbon** [ká:rbn]

24 **astronomer** [əstránəmər]

26 **reasonably** [rí:znəbli]

26 **conceive of ...**

27 **... degrees centigrade**

27 **... degrees Fahrenheit**

33 **barely** [béərli]

33 **permanently** [pə́:rmənəntli]

36 **retain** [ritéin]

入試発展レベル（二次・有名私大）

2 **burn** *oneself* **out**

2 **swiftly** [swíftli]

4 **exhaust** *oneself*

6 **boil away**

11 **refine** [rifáin]

12 **assessment** [əsésmənt]

13 **habitability** [hæ̀bətəbíləti]

14 **Venus** [ví:nəs]

20 **hold on to ...**

20 **disastrous** [dizǽstrəs]

21 **evaporate** [ivǽpərèit]

26 **fierce** [fíərs]

28 **lead** [léd]（名）

28 **atmospheric pressure**

29 **withstand** [wiðstǽnd]

32 **disturbing** [distə́:rbiŋ]（形）

32 **probe** [próub]

32 **hopefully** [hóupfəli]

33 **shut down**

35 **farther** [fá:rðər]

37 **waste** [wéist]（名）

その他

2 **radiate** [réidièit]（動）　放射する、発する

5 **orbit** [ɔ́:rbət]（動）　軌道を描いて回る

8 **astrophysicist** [æ̀stroufízisist]
　　　　　天体物理学者、宇宙物理学者

9 **uninhabitable** [ʌ̀ninhǽbətəbl]
　　　　　居住に適さない、住めない

17 **orbital distance**　軌道距離

21 **hydrogen atom**　水素原子

22 **oxygen atom**　酸素原子

22 **dense atmosphere**　濃い大気

23 **stifling** [stáifliŋ]　息が詰まるような

24 **harbor** [há:rbər]（動）　かくまう、心に抱く

24 **padded** [pǽdəd]　詰め物をした（ような）

27 **roasting** [róustiŋ]（形）　焼き付くように暑い

31 **radar imagery**　レーダー画像

32 **unmanned** [ʌnmǽnd]　無人の

35 **frigidly** [frídʒidli]　冷たく、冷淡に

36 **congenial** [kəndʒí:njəl]　心地よい

36 **usable** [jú:zəbl]　使用に適した、使用可能な

段落要旨　　各段落のまとめとなるように、空所に適切な語句を入れなさい。（同じ番号には、同じ語句が入ります）

展開	段落	要旨
主題の提示	1	地球が、適切な大きさの（①　　　　　　）から、適切な距離の軌道を回転しているので、我々は存在できている。
主題の展開①	2	我々の（②　　　　　）に適した領域は、地球が現在より（①　　　　　　）に 5% 近いところから 15% 遠いところまでの、狭い範囲だと計算されている。
主題の展開②	3	（③　　　　　　）は大きさと組成の面で地球と似ているが、（①　　　　　　）にわずかに近いために生命が（②　　　　　）できない過酷な環境となった。
主題の展開③	4	（①　　　　　　）から遠い（④　　　　　　）は、使用可能な大気を保持できず、極寒の氷原と化した。

百字要約　　「段落要旨」を参考にして、本文全体の内容を百字程度の日本語で要約しなさい。

（下書き）

　　　　　　　　　　　　　　　　　　　　　10　　　　　　　　　　　　　　　　　　　　20

　　　　　　　　　　　　　　　　　　　　　10　　　　　　　　　　　　　　　　　　　　20

本文解説

1 【仮定法：if が省略された条件節】

(l.3) **Had our sun been** ten times as massive, it **would have exhausted** itself after ten million years instead of ten billion and we wouldn't be here now.

(l.8) In 1978, an astrophysicist named Michael Hart made some calculations and concluded that Earth **would have been** uninhabitable / **had it been** just 1 percent farther from or 5 percent closer to the Sun.

> ▶ 仮定法で条件節の if を省略すると、主語と動詞（または助動詞）の位置が倒置する。Had our sun been ten times as massive = If our sun had been ten times as massive
> had it been just 1 percent farther from or 5 percent closer to the Sun = if it had been just 1 percent farther from or 5 percent closer to the Sun
> *ex.* Were I in his position, I would accept the offer.
> 「私が彼の立場にあれば、その申し出を受けるのに」

2 【仮定法：if 節に相当する語句】

(l.6) **Too much nearer and** everything on Earth would have boiled away. **Much farther away and** everything would have frozen.

> ▶ どちらの文も and の前の句に仮定の意味が含まれている。If we had been too much nearer, everything on Earth would have boiled away. / If we had been much farther away, everything would have frozen. の意味。（地球の位置が現在も変わらないという視点に立てば、If we were too much nearer, ... / If we were much farther away, ... なども可能だろう。）

3 【make all the difference】【how it turns out】

(l.16) In size and composition, Venus is very like Earth, but the small difference in orbital distance **made all the difference to how it turned out**.

> ▶ make a difference「（主語が）相違を生ずる、影響を与える」 make all the difference to ...「…に大きな違いを生じさせる、…の状況を一変させる」 ここは「軌道距離のわずかな差で、事の結果がまったく違ってしまった」の意味。*ex.* It makes no difference whether you have experience or not.「経験のあるなしは関係ありません」
> ▶ how it turns out「その結果」 turn out ...「…になる、…に進展する」は、…の部分に名詞、不定詞、形容詞、副詞、that 節などを伴う。 *ex.* Everything turned out all right.「万事うまくいった」

4 【文構造】【too+ 形容詞 +a[an]+ 可算名詞】

(l.23) Although people of my age will recall a time when astronomers hoped that Venus might harbor life beneath its padded clouds, possibly even a kind of tropical vegetation, // we now know that it is much **too fierce an environment** for any kind of life that we can reasonably conceive of.

> ▶ Although で始まる節は tropical vegetation まで。when ... tropical vegetation は a time を説明する関係副詞節。possibly even a kind of tropical vegetation は harbor life「生命を隠している」の life の補足で、「ひょっとするとある種の熱帯植物さえも」。
> ▶ too fierce an environment for ...「…にとっては過酷すぎる環境」 直前の much は too を強調している。too fierce an environment の語順にも注意。a very fierce environment や such a fierce environment とほぼ同意だが、〈too+ 形容詞 +a[an]+ 可算名詞〉の語順になる。
> *ex.* It was too cold a day for swimming in the sea.「海で泳ぐには寒すぎる日だった」
> ▶ for any kind of life that we can reasonably conceive of の that は関係代名詞。 conceive of ...「…を考え出す、想像する」 全体で「我々が合理的に考え得るいかなる種類の生命にとっても」。

Memo

CD 1
🎧 66

Overflowing with more information than we can possibly hold in our heads, we're increasingly handing off the job of remembering to search engines and smartphones. Google is even reportedly working on eyeglasses that could one day recognize faces and supply details about whoever you're looking at. But new research shows that outsourcing* our memory — and expecting that information will be continually and quickly available — is changing our memorizing habits.

🎧 67

Research conducted by Betsy Sparrow, an assistant professor of psychology at Columbia University, has identified (1)three new realities about how we process information in the Internet age. First, her experiments showed that when we don't know the answer to a question, we now think about where we can find the nearest web connection instead of the subject of the question itself. For example, the question "Are there any countries with only one color in their flag?" prompted study participants to think not about flags but about computers.

🎧 68

A second revelation: when we expect to be able to find information again later on, we don't remember it as well as when we think it might become unavailable. (2)Sparrow's participants were asked to type facts into a computer — for example, "The space shuttle Columbia broke up during re-entry* over Texas in February 2003." Half were told that their work would be saved; the rest were told that their words would be wiped out. Those who believed that the computer would store the information recalled details less well on their own. Sparrow compares their situation to one we all experience in the real world: "Since search engines are continually available to us, we may often be in a state of not feeling we need to remember the information internally. When we need it, we will look it up." Sound familiar?

🎧 69

The researcher's final observation: the expectation that we'll be able to find information regularly leads us to form a memory not of the fact itself but of where we'll be able to find it. "We are learning what the computer 'knows' and when we should pay attention to where we have stored information in our computer-based memories," Sparrow concluded in her report. "We are becoming closely related to our computer tools."

Before you grow nervous about turning into a cyborg*, however, you should know that this new relation with our digital devices is really just a variation of a much more familiar phenomenon, what psychologists call (3)transactive memory. This is the unspoken arrangement by which groups of people give memory tasks to each individual, with information to be shared when needed. In a marriage, one parent might remember the kids' afterschool appointments while the other keeps track of the recycling pickup schedule. In a workplace team, one member may deal with data and calculations while ₃₅ a colleague is charged with remembering client preferences.

✎70   The way we assign tasks to our computers is simply an extension of this principle — an instance of transactive memory carried out on a very grand scale. But ₍₄₎this handoff comes with a disadvantage. Skills like critical thinking and analysis must develop in the context of facts: we need something to think and reason about, after all. And these ₄₀ facts can't be Googled as we go; they need to be stored in the original hard drive, our long-term memory. Especially in the case of children, "(X) must precede (Y)," says Daniel Willingham, a professor of psychology at the University of Virginia, meaning that the days of drilling the multiplication table* and memorizing the names of the Presidents aren't over quite yet. Adults, too, need to recruit a supply of stored knowledge in order ₄₅ to situate and judge new information they encounter. ₍₅₎You can't Google context.

* outsourcing「外部に仕事を依頼すること」 re-entry「(宇宙船の大気圏への) 再突入」 cyborg「サイボーグ」
   multiplication table「九九の表」

1   ・
         ....
         ....
         ・
         ....
         ....
         ・
         ....
         ....

2 実験の内容：..
         ....
       実験の結果：..
         ....

3   10   20

4 ....

5 ....   **6** ....   **7** ....

語句　音声は、「英語」→「日本語の意味」の順で読まれます。　CD 1- Tr 71-74

入試基礎レベル

19 **recall** [rikɔ́:l]

20 **compare ... to ~**

22 **look ... up**

25 **form** [fɔ́:rm] （動）

26 **pay attention to ...**

28 **conclude** [kənklú:d]

28 **(be) related to ...**

29 **turn into ...**

32 **arrangement** [əréindʒmənt]

35 **deal with ...**

38 **instance** [ínstəns]

38 **carry out ...**

39 **skill** [skíl]

45 **supply** [səplái] （名）

入試標準レベル（共通テスト・私大）

3 **reportedly** [ripɔ́:rtidli]

7 **conduct** [kəndʌ́kt] （動）

7 **psychology** [saikálədʒi]

8 **identify** [aidéntəfài]

8 **process** [prá:ses] （動）

11 **subject** [sʌ́bdʒikt] （名）

12 **participant** [pɑːrtísəpənt]

17 **break up**

18 **the rest**

19 **store** [stɔ́:r] （動）

24 **observation** [àbsərvéiʃən]

30 **digital device**

31 **psychologist** [saikálədʒist]

35 **calculation** [kælkjəléiʃən]

36 **colleague** [káli:g]

36 **be charged with ...**

36 **client** [kláiənt]

37 **assign ... to ~**

37 **extension** [eksténʃən]

37 **principle** [prínsəpl]

39 **come with ...**

39 **analysis** [ənǽləsis]

40 **in the context of ...**

42 **in the case of ...**

45 **be over**　終わって、済んで

46 **encounter** [enkáuntər]

46 **context** [kántekst]

入試発展レベル（二次・有名私大）

1 **can possibly** *do*

2 **hand off ... to ~**

5 **continually** [kəntínjuəli]

12 **prompt ... to** *do*

14 **revelation** [rèvəléiʃən]

21 **be in a state of ...**

22 **internally** [intɔ́:rnli]

25 **lead ... to** *do*

30 **variation of ...**

36 **preference** [préfərəns]

39 **handoff** [hǽndɔ̀(:)f]

39 **critical thinking**

42 **factual** [fǽktʃuəl]

44 **drill** [dríl] （動）

45 **recruit** [rikrú:t]

46 **situate** [sítʃuèit]

その他

4 **details**　〔複数形で〕詳細

4 **outsourcing** [àutsɔ́:siŋ]　外部委託

17 **re-entry**　（大気圏への）再突入

18 **wipe out ...**　（データなどを）消去する

29 **grow nervous about ...**　…に神経質になる

29 **cyborg** [sáibɔ̀:rg]　サイボーグ

31 **transactive memory**　交換記憶

34 **keep track of ...**　〜の記録をつける

41 **hard drive**　ハードディスク

44 **multiplication table**　掛け算表、九九の表

展開	段落	要旨
主題の提示	1	検索エンジンなどへの記憶の（①　　　　　　　）が、私たちの記憶（②　　　　　　　）の変化を招いている。
研究結果と分析①	2	ある研究で3つの新事実が確認された。まず、私たちは質問の答えがわからないとき、質問の（③　　　　　）ではなく、ネット接続が可能な場所を考えることがわかった。
研究結果と分析②	3	2つ目は、後でまた（④　　　　　）が入手可能だという期待があると、それをよく記憶していないということ。
研究結果と分析③	4	最後は、（④　　　　　）がいつでも入手できると期待することで、それを見つけられる場所についての記憶を形成すること。
展開	5	しかし、（⑤　　　　　　）との新たな関係は「（⑥　　　　　）記憶」にすぎない。それは記憶課題を各個人に委託し、必要なときに（④　　　　　）を共有するものである。
結論	6	だが、分析などの技能は事実の（⑦　　　　　）の中で発達させなければならない。また、これに必要な事実は、人間の（⑧　　　　　）記憶に蓄積されている必要がある。（⑦　　　　　）はグーグル検索できないのである。

（下書き）　　　　　　　　　　　　　　　10　　　　　　　　　　　　　　　20

（空欄の原稿用紙マス目）

10　　　　　　　　　　　　　　　20

（空欄の原稿用紙マス目）

本文解説

1 【文修飾の副詞】

(l.3)　Google is even **reportedly** working on eyeglasses that could one day recognize faces and supply details about whoever you're looking at.

> ▶ reportedly は「伝えられるところによれば、うわさによれば」の意味で、文全体を修飾する副詞 (sentence adverb) である。It is reported that Google is even working ... と書き換えることができる。Reportedly, Google is even working ... のように文頭に置かれることもある。英英辞典は "according to what some people say (but you have no direct evidence of it)" と説明している。
> *ex.* More than two hundred people were reportedly killed in the past week's fighting.
> 「伝えられるところでは、先週の戦闘で 200 人以上が死亡したもようだ」
> ▶ allegedly も reportedly と同様の意味で、どちらも新聞などで多用される副詞である。
> *ex.* He allegedly spread false information to boost share prices of his company.
> 「伝えられるところでは、彼は自分の会社の株価を上げるために偽情報を広めたとのことである」

2 【not ... but 〜】

(l.11)　For example, the question "Are there any countries with only one color in their flag?" prompted study participants to think **not about** flags **but about** computers.

(l.24)　The researcher's final observation: the expectation that we'll be able to find information regularly leads us to form a memory **not of** the fact itself **but of** where we'll be able to find it.

> ▶ どちらの文も not ... but 〜「…ではなく〜」が使われ、それぞれ同じ前置詞が続いている。think about ... , a memory of ... が基本なので、to think not about flags but (think) about computers, to form a memory not of the fact itself but (a memory) of where we'll be able to find it と、省略を補って読む。

3 【疑問詞で始まる節】

(l.26)　"We are learning **what** the computer 'knows' and **when** we should pay attention to **where** we have stored information in our computer-based memories," Sparrow concluded in her report.

> ▶ learning の目的語は what ... と when ... の 2 つの節で、それぞれ疑問詞で始まる名詞節である。また when 以下の部分で where ... の節は前置詞 to の目的語で、where は疑問詞あるいは、先行詞が省略された関係副詞と考える。
> ▶ 全体で「私たちはコンピュータが何を『知っているか』、また、コンピュータをベースとした記憶の中のどこに情報を保管しているか［情報を保管している場所］についていつ注意を払うべきかを学んでいるのです」。

4 【同格】【transactive memory】

(l.29)　Before you grow nervous about turning into a cyborg, however, you should know that this new relation with our digital devices is really just a variation of a much more familiar phenomenon, **what psychologists call transactive memory**.

> ▶ what psychologists call transactive memory は、直前の a variation of a much more familiar phenomenon「私たちにずっとなじみ深い現象の 1 つの変種」と同格で、「（つまり）心理学者が交換記憶と呼ぶもの」の意味。

▶ transactive memory「交換記憶」とは、1985 年に Daniel Wegner が唱え始めた心理学的仮説で、「誰が、何を知っているかを認識すること」と定義されている。ひとりですべての情報を記憶するのではなく、誰が、何を知っているかを記憶することで、認知的な負担が軽減され、パフォーマンスの促進につながると指摘されている。

▶ grow nervous about ...「…に関して神経質になる」 cyborg「サイボーグ」は cybernetic organism「自動制御系技術の生命体」の略で、英英辞典には "In science fiction, a cyborg is a being that is part human and part machine, or a machine that looks like a human being." とある。variation of ...「…の変種、変形」

5　【by which】【with の用法】

(l.31)　This is the unspoken arrangement / **by which** groups of people give memory tasks to each individual, **with** information to be shared when needed.

▶ 〈前置詞＋関係代名詞〉がある文は、まずその前で区切り、続く部分は関係代名詞の先行詞を補って読む。ここでは which の先行詞は the unspoken arrangement なので、This is the unspoken arrangement「これは暗黙の取り決めである」+ by the unspoken arrangement groups of people give memory tasks to each individual「その暗黙の取り決めによって、集団が記憶課題を各個人に委託する」と読む。

▶ with 以下は、直前の groups of people give memory tasks to each individual を補足して、「必要なときには、情報を共有できるようにして」の意味。with ... は〈with + O(information) + C(to be shared)〉で付帯状況を表す用法。 when needed は when it is needed の省略で it は information を指すが、具体的には「与えられた記憶課題により各個人が持っている情報」を意味する。

6　【reason】【形容詞的用法の to 不定詞】

(l.39)　Skills like critical thinking and analysis must develop in the context of facts: we need something **to think and reason about**, after all.

▶ reason はここでは動詞で、"to form a particular judgment about a situation after carefully considering the facts" の意味。

▶ to think and reason about は something を修飾する形容詞的用法の to 不定詞。think about something「何かについて思考する」+ reason about something「何かについて論理的に考える［判断する］」→ something to think and reason about「思考し、論理的に考えるための何か」

7　【meaning ...】

(l.42)　Especially in the case of children, "factual knowledge must precede skill," says Daniel Willingham, a professor of psychology at the University of Virginia, **meaning** that the days of drilling the multiplication table and memorizing the names of the Presidents aren't over quite yet.

▶ meaning that ... は分詞構文で、and it means that ... あるいは , which means ... の意味。その it や which は前の Especially in the case of children, "factual knowledge must precede skill," を受けている。「特に子どもの場合は『事実に関する知識は技能に先んじなくてはならない』、つまり…という意味である」

Charles Darwin had more in common with chimpanzees than even he realized. 🔊 1
Before he was universally known for his theory of natural selection, the young naturalist
made a decision that has long been praised as the type of behavior that fundamentally
separates humans from other apes.

5   In 1858, before Darwin published *On the Origin of Species*, his friend Alfred Russel 🔊 2
Wallace mailed Darwin his own theory of evolution that closely matched what Darwin
had secretly been working on for more than two decades. Instead of racing to publish
and ignoring Wallace's work, Darwin included Wallace's outline alongside his own
abstract★ so that the two could be presented jointly before the Linnean Society★ the
10 following month. "I would far rather burn my whole book than that Wallace or any man
should think that (1)I had behaved in a paltry★ spirit," Darwin wrote.

   This kind of behavior, seeking to benefit others and promote cooperation, has now 🔊 3
been found in chimps, the species that Darwin did more than any other human to
connect us with. In the study, published in a major scientific journal, primatologist★
15 Frans de Waal and his colleagues presented chimps with (2)a simplified version of the
choice that Darwin faced.

   Pairs of chimps were brought into a testing room where they were separated only by 🔊 4
a wire mesh. On one side was a bucket containing 30 tokens★ that the chimpanzee could
give to an experimenter for a food reward. Half of the tokens were of one color that
20 resulted in only the chimpanzee that gave the token receiving a reward. The other tokens
were of a different color that resulted in both chimpanzees receiving a food reward. If
chimpanzees were motivated only by selfish interests, they would be expected to choose
a reward only for themselves (or it should be 50-50 if they were choosing randomly).
But individuals were significantly more likely to choose the cooperative option.

25   De Waal says that (3)previous studies showing chimps to be selfish may have been 🔊 5
poorly designed. "The chimps had to understand a complex food delivery system," De
Waal wrote, "and were often placed so far apart that they may not have realized how
their actions benefited others." De Waal added that his study does not rule out the
possibility that chimpanzees were influenced by reciprocal exchanges outside the

experimental setting such as grooming* or social support.   30

6   (4)<u>This latter possibility</u> offers exciting research opportunities for the future.
Chimpanzee society, like the greater scientific community that studies them, is built
around such mutual exchanges. Science is a social activity, and sharing the rewards
from one another's research allows scientists to improve their work over time. Like the
chimpanzees he would connect us with, Darwin recognized the utility of (5)<u>sharing   35
rewards with others</u>.

* abstract「概要、要約」 the Linnean Society「リンネ協会（博物学の定期刊行物を出版する英国の組織）」
  paltry「卑しい、けちな」 primatologist「霊長類学者」 tokens「代用コイン」 grooming「毛づくろい」

解答欄

1
....
....

2 （ア）
....
....
　（イ）
....
....

3
....

4
....
....

5
....

6
....

語句 音声は、「英語」→「日本語の意味」の順で読まれます。　　　CD 2 - Tr 7-10

入試基礎レベル

3 **make a decision** ....

3 **praise** [préiz] (動) ....

6 **mail** [méil] (動) ....

8 **include** [inklú:d] ....

11 **behave** [bihéiv] ....

12 **benefit** [bénəfit] (動) ....

12 **promote** [prəmóut] ....

13 **species** [spí:ʃi:z] ....

18 **contain** [kəntéin] ....

19 **reward** [riwɔ́:rd] (名) ....

20 **result in ...** ....

24 **individual** [ìndəvídʒuəl] (名) ....

26 **delivery** [dilívəri] ....

27 **place** [pléis] (動) ....

28 **add** [ǽd] ....

29 **influence** [ínfluəns] (動) ....

29 **exchange** [ikstʃéindʒ] (名) ....

31 **opportunity** [àpərtú:nəti] ....

33 **share** [ʃéər] (動) ....

34 **allow ... to *do*** ....

34 **improve** [imprú:v] ....

入試標準レベル（共通テスト・私大）

1 **have ... in common with ~** ....

2 **universally** [jù:nivɔ́:rsəli] ....

3 **fundamentally** [fʌ̀ndəméntəli] ....

4 **separate ... from ~** ....

4 **ape** [éip] ....

8 **ignore** [ignɔ́:r] ....

9 **present** [prizént] (動) ....

12 **cooperation** [kouàpəréiʃən] ....

15 **colleague** [káli:g] ....

15 **present ... with ~** ....

22 **motivate** [móutəvèit] ....

23 **randomly** [rǽndəmli] ....

24 **significantly** [signífikəntli] ....

24 **cooperative** [kouápərətiv] ....

24 **option** [ápʃən] ....

25 **previous** [prí:viəs] ....

26 **complex** [kampléks] ....

27 **apart** [əpá:rt] ....

33 **mutual** [mjú:tʃuəl] ....

入試発展レベル（二次・有名私大）

2 **theory of natural selection** ....

6 **theory of evolution** ....

7 **race to *do*** ....

8 **alongside ...** ....

12 **seek to *do*** ....

15 **simplify** [símpləfài] ....

28 **rule out ...** ....

35 **utility** [ju:tíləti] ....

その他

2 **naturalist** [nǽtʃərəlist]　博物学者

5 ***On the Origin of Species***

　　　『種の起源』

9 **abstract** [ǽbstrækt] (名) 概要、要約

11 **paltry** [pɔ́:ltri]　卑しい、けちな

14 **primatologist** [praimətálədʒist]

　　　霊長類学者

18 **wire mesh**　金網

18 **token** [tóukn]　代用コイン、代用貨幣

19 **experimenter** [ikspérəmèntər]

　　　実験者

29 **reciprocal** [risíprəkəl]　相互の、お返しの

30 **grooming** [grú:miŋ]　毛づくろい

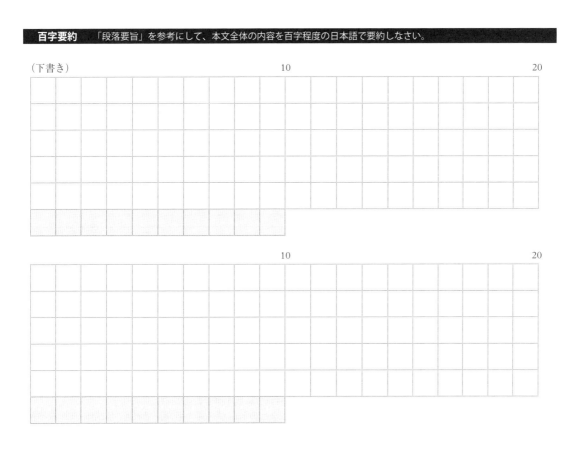

段落要旨 各段落のまとめとなるように、空所に適切な語句を入れなさい。（同じ番号には、同じ語句が入ります）

展開	段落	要旨
導入	1	ダーウィンと（①　　　　　　　　）には多くの共通点があった。
展開①	2	ダーウィンは『（②　　　　　　　　）』を出版する際、友人の功績も併せて公表した。
展開②	3	他人を益して（③　　　　　　）を促す行動が、（①　　　　　　　　）に見つかっている。
展開③	4	（①　　　　　　　　）はある実験で、仲間もほうびをもらえる（③　　　　　　）的な行動を見せた。
展開④	5	今回の実験とは異なる結果を示した過去の研究は、設定が不備だった可能性がある。また、今回の実験結果は、実験での設定とは異なる（④　　　　　　）に影響を受けた可能性もある。
結論	6	（④　　　　　　）を中心に構築される（①　　　　　　　　）の社会と同様に、科学界も互いに得たものを共有することが有益な社会活動である。ダーウィンはその有益性を認識していたのだ。

百字要約 「段落要旨」を参考にして、本文全体の内容を百字程度の日本語で要約しなさい。

（下書き）　　　　　　　　　　　　　　　　　10　　　　　　　　　　　　　　　　　20

10　　　　　　　　　　　　　　　　　20

本文解説

1 【文構造】

(l.7)　Instead of **racing** to publish and **ignoring** Wallace's work, Darwin included Wallace's outline alongside his own abstract **so that** the two could be presented jointly **before** the Linnean Society the following month.

> ▶ Instead of に続く 2 つの動名詞 racing, ignoring の意味上の主語は Darwin。
>
> ▶ so that the two could be presented は目的を表し、「2 つを提出できるように」。before は「（判断、審理などのために）…の前に、面前に」の意味。

2 【would (far) rather ... than 〜】

(l.10)　"I **would far rather** burn my whole book **than that** Wallace or any man should think that I had behaved in a paltry spirit," Darwin wrote.

> ▶ would (far) rather ... than 〜 は「〜よりむしろ（はるかに）…したい」の意味で、far は rather を強めている。この文では ... に動詞句 burn my whole book が、〜 には that Wallace ... spirit という節が置かれて、その両者が比べられている。would rather の直後に節が続く場合、節の中は通常仮定法過去で、初めに that はつけない。
>> *cf.* I would rather go somewhere else for dinner.「夕食はどこか別の場所で食べたい」
>> I'd rather you didn't smoke.「できればタバコを吸ってほしくない」

3 【倒置】

(l.18)　**On one side** (V)**was** (S)**a bucket** containing 30 tokens that the chimpanzee could give to an experimenter for a food reward.

> ▶ On one side という副詞句が文頭に置かれたために、主部 a bucket ... reward と動詞 was が倒置されている。普通の語順 A bucket containing 30 tokens that the chimpanzee could give to an experimenter for a food reward was on one side. よりはるかにバランスがいい文になっている。

4 【of の用法】【動名詞の意味上の主語】

(l.19)　Half of the tokens were **of** one **color** that resulted **in** only **the chimpanzee** that gave the token **receiving** a reward.

(l.20)　The other tokens were of a different color that resulted **in** both **chimpanzees receiving** a food reward.

> ▶ 〈of ＋名詞〉で「…のある、…の性質を持つ」の意味の形容詞句になるものがある。of one color は「ある色をしている」、of a different color で「別な色をしている」の意味。
>> *ex.* This information may be of use to us some time in the future.
>> 「この情報はいつか私たちに役立つかもしれない」
>> When I was (of) your age, children knew to respect their parents.
>> 「僕が君の年のときは、子どもというものは両親を尊敬すべきだと知っていたよ」
>> 2 つ目の例のように、age, color, shape, size などの名詞が〈of ＋名詞〉で叙述的に用いられるとき、of が省略されることもある。
>
> ▶ result in ... は「…という結果になる、…に終わる」。2 つの動詞 receiving は前置詞 in の目的語だが、意味上の主語はそれぞれ the chimpanzee, chimpanzees である。resulted in 以下の意味はそれぞれ「そのコインを渡したチンパンジーだけがほうびをもらえる結果になる」、「両方のチンパンジーがほうびに食べ物をもらえる結果になる」。
>> *ex.* We are looking forward to the truth coming out.（the truth が coming out の意味上の主語）
>> 「私たちは真実が明らかにされるのを心待ちにしている」

Memo

Should the government have more control over people's lives? Most people who are advocates of democracy believe emphatically that the government should not. (1)Such people believe that everyone should be free to make their own choices and live their lives as they please and do so uninhibited by higher authorities. Recently, however, some
5 economists have argued that the government should play a greater role in people's lives. These economists believe that governments can intervene in ways that greatly benefit society and still protect basic democratic values.

In 2017, economist Richard Thaler received the Nobel Prize in Economics for his work in the field of "behavioral economics." Thaler and his collaborators argued that
10 (2)traditional economic theories of how people behave are not fully accurate because they fail to account for how people actually behave. They explain that traditional economic theories are based on the belief that people act "rationally" and make all of their decisions on the basis of what is best for them economically. On the contrary, Thaler's research has shown that people do not, in fact, act "rationally" and instead make many choices
15 that are not the best in some aspects of life. For example, despite hundreds of scientific studies showing that smoking cigarettes is unhealthy and dangerous, millions of people continue to smoke. The reason people continue to smoke despite the harmful consequences is because the effects of smoking are far away in the future. People may become sick or die from smoking, but it will happen many years later. The effects are so
20 distant that smokers cannot perceive them now. Thaler's work has shown that if the effects were more immediate, people would be more likely to avoid smoking.

Many behavioral economists like Thaler believe in an approach called "libertarian paternalism." This means that governments and authorities should allow people to live their lives as they please but that they should also give them incentives to do what is in
25 their best interest. In other words, (3)governments should "nudge" people to make better choices. In fact, Thaler and his colleague Cass Sunstein published a book titled *Nudge: Improving Decisions about Health, Wealth, and Happiness*. In this book, they provide many examples of how governments, universities, and other institutions can "nudge" their members to act in different (i.e. better) ways. For example, one study revealed that
30 people eat different foods depending on the order in which food is displayed to them. If a cafeteria manager places unhealthy food before healthy food, people are more likely to consume the unhealthy food. However, if he or she (4)does the opposite, diners will choose the healthier options. Therefore, it is in the best interest of diners, cafeteria managers, and institutions to place healthy food before unhealthy food.

35 Thaler and Sunstein argue that governments and other institutions should be

required to adopt these policies in the best interest of society. They advocated for policies based on "libertarian paternalism" to achieve this.

🖜15   The organization of food in a cafeteria is not a controversial issue. However, some people have challenged other aspects of "libertarian paternalism" by suggesting that it violates democratic principles of people's rights to choose what is best for themselves. (5)<u>These critics argue that requiring "libertarian paternalism" is unfair</u> because it forces people to do things they would not otherwise do. The fact that such policies would be "paternalistic," meaning that they would require something, violates the "libertarian" aspect. For example, New York City politicians proposed a law that would prohibit the sale of soda larger than 0.47 liters. Since soda is unhealthy (it causes tooth problems, is linked to weight gain, and can cause diabetes, among many other problems), politicians believed prohibiting the sale of large quantities of soda would help make their city population healthier. However, critics proclaimed that this went against democratic principles that declare people should have freedom to buy what they want. They argued, "If I want to buy a big soda, I should have the right to buy a big soda!" The soda policy was ultimately abandoned, but its effect on politics still remains pertinent today.

🖜16   Should the government adopt "libertarian paternalism" as a policy guideline? There is much ongoing debate concerning this proposal. Proponents believe it will make society better at a minimal cost, while opponents believe that it violates the basic principles of (A). Although the discussion continues, "libertarian paternalism" is definitely worth considering as a possible policy solution to some of today's problems.

解答欄

1
....

....

2 a) ....

....

b) ....

....

3 ....

4 ....

5 ....

6 ....

語句　　音声は、「英語」→「日本語の意味」の順で読まれます。　　　　　CD 2- Tr 17-20

入試基礎レベル

5　play a ... role in ～

6　benefit [bénəfit] (動)

13　on the basis of ...

14　instead [instéd]

20　perceive [pərsíːv]

21　immediate [imíːdiət]

21　be likely to *do*

22　approach [əpróutʃ] (名)

23　allow O to *do*

30　depending on ...

30　display [displéi] (動)

36　policy [páləsi]

37　achieve [ətʃíːv]

38　organization [ɔ̀ːrgənəzéiʃən]

38　issue [íʃuː]

41　force O to *do*

45　be linked to ...

54　opponent [əpóunənt]

入試標準レベル（共通テスト・私大）

2　democracy [dimákrəsi]

5　economist [ikánəmist]

10　accurate [ǽkjərət]

11　fail to *do*

11　account for ...

13　economically [èkənámikəli]

13　on the contrary

18　consequence [kánsəkwèns]

25　in other words

26　colleague [káliːg]

27　institution [ìnstət(j)úːʃən]

32　consume [kəns(j)úːm]

33　option [ápʃən]

36　adopt [ədápt]

39　aspect [ǽspekt]

40　principle [prínsəpl]

44　politician [pàlətíʃən]

44　prohibit [prouhíbət]

47　large quantities of ...

48　go against ...

49　declare [dikléər]

51　abandon [əbǽndən]

53　concerning ...

56　definitely [défənətli]

56　worth *doing*

56　solution to ...

入試発展レベル（二次・有名私大）

2　advocate [ǽdvəkət] (名)

4　as A pleases

4　higher authorities　　　より上位の権力

6　intervene [ìntərvíːn]

12　rationally [rǽʃənəli]

24　incentive [inséntiv]

25　in *one's* best interest

36　advocate for ...

38　controversial [kàntrəvə́ːrʃəl]

40　violate [váiəlèit]

41　critic [krítik]

48　population [pàpjəléiʃən]

51　ultimately [ʌ́ltəmətli]

その他

2　emphatically [emfǽtikəli]　断固として、力強く

4　uninhibited [ʌ̀ninhíbətid]
　　　　　　　　　（行動などが）制約されない

8　the Nobel Prize in Economics
　　　　　　　　　ノーベル経済学賞

9　behavioral economics　行動経済学

9　collaborator [kəlǽbərèitər] 共同研究者、協力者

25　nudge [nʌ́dʒ]
　　　　　そっと肘で突く、優しく促す［説得する］

29　i.e.　　　　　すなわち、つまり

32　diner [dáinər]　　食事をする人

39　challenge [tʃǽlindʒ]
　　　…（意見・考えなど）について異議を唱える

43　paternalistic [pətə̀ːrnəlístik]
　　　　　　　家父長的な、パターナリズム的

46　diabetes [dàiəbíːtiz]　糖尿病

48　proclaim [proukléim]　公言する、はっきり言う

51　pertinent [pə́ːrtənənt]（密接な）関連［関係］のある

53　ongoing [ángòuiŋ] (形)　進行中の

53　proponent [prəpóunənt]　支持者、擁護者

54　minimal [mínəməl]　最小限の

展開	段落	要旨
主題の提示	1	大半の（①　　　　　　　　　）支持者は、政府は人々の生活に介入すべきではないと考えている。一方で、政府は人々の生活により大きな役割を果たすべきだと主張する経済学者もいる。
主題の展開①	2	行動経済学者のセイラーは、人々が「（②　　　　　　　）」に行動することを前提とした伝統的な経済理論は、完全には正確なものでないと主張した。彼は、人々は最善でない選択をすることが多いという研究結果を示した。
主題の展開②	3	多くの行動経済学者は、人々によりよい選択をするよう（③　　　　　　）を与える「リバタリアン・パターナリズム」のアプローチを支持している。研究によると、食べ物が並んでいる順番次第で人々の食べるものは変わるので、店が健康的な食べ物を前に置くとすべての人の利益になる、ということはその一例である。
主題の展開③	4	セイラーらは「リバタリアン・パターナリズム」に基づく政策を主張した。
主題の展開④	5	「リバタリアン・パターナリズム」の批判者は、（④　　　　　　）されなければしないようなことを人々に強いることは不公平だと主張する。一定量を超える炭酸飲料の販売を禁じる法案が提案されたときも、批判者たちは、それは（①　　　　　　　）の原則に反すると主張した。
結論	6	政府が「リバタリアン・パターナリズム」を採用すべきかどうかの議論は今も続いているが、今日の問題への政治的解決策として検討する価値はある。

（下書き）　　　　　　　　　　　　　　　　　　　　　10　　　　　　　　　　　　　　　　　　　　20

10　　　　　　　　　　　　　　　　　　　　20

本文解説

1　【on the contrary】

(l.13)　**On the contrary**, Thaler's research has shown that people do not, in fact, act "rationally" and instead make many choices that are not the best in some aspects of life.

- ▶ on the contrary は「それどころか、むしろ、その逆で」の意味で、前述の強い否定（＝ a strong denial of the previous statement）を表す。ここも言い換えると、"Actually, the opposite is the case. Thaler's research has shown that ... " となる。
  - *ex.* I am not against his plan. On the contrary, I am in favor of it.
    「私は彼の計画に反対ではありません。それどころか、大賛成ですよ」
- ▶ 似た形の on the other hand は「その一方、別の見方をすれば」の意味で、単に 2 つの事柄、考えや視点を対照する場合（＝ introduces a contrast, without claiming which side carries the most weight）に用いる。
  - *ex.* He was too obstinate, but on the other hand he was reliable.
    「彼は強情すぎるが、他方では頼りになった」

2　【The reason ... is because 〜】

(l.17)　**The reason** people continue to smoke despite the harmful consequences **is because** the effects of smoking are far away in the future.

- ▶ The reason (why) ... is because 〜 で「…の理由は〜だ」の意味を表す。この文では、the reason の後ろに関係副詞 why が省略されている。because 以下は、is の補語の働きをしている名詞節である。
- ▶ The reason (why) ... is に続く節は that 節とするのが正しいとされるが、上記のように because 節が用いられることも多い。
  - *ex.* The reason I want to be a doctor is that I would like to help people.
    「私が医者になりたい理由は、人を助けたいからだ」

3　【文構造】【otherwise の用法】

(l.41)　These critics argue that requiring "libertarian paternalism" is unfair because it forces people to do things they would not **otherwise** do.

- ▶ because 以下は because it (= "libertarian paternalism") forces people to do things that they (= people) would not otherwise do の意味で、things の後ろに関係代名詞 that[which] が省略されている。〈force O to *do*〉で「O に無理やり〜させる」。otherwise は「もしそうでなければ」の意味で、この文では「もし『リバタリアン・パターナリズム』が人々に強制しなければ」を 1 語で表現している。全体で「『リバタリアン・パターナリズム』は、強制されなければしないようなことを人々に強制的にさせるので」。
- ▶ otherwise は、原義は「別 (other) のやり方で (wise)」。大きく 3 つの用法がある。
  1)「もしそうでなければ (if not)」：文頭に置かれ文全体を修飾することが多いが、上記の例のように would, could などの助動詞の後に置かれ、文中で仮定法の文脈で使われることもある。
  - *ex.* You'd better quit smoking. Otherwise, you might get cancer.
    「喫煙やめた方がいい。さもないと、がんになるかもしれないよ」
    The medicine has helped many athletes to recover from serious injuries that would otherwise have seen them retire from sports.
    「その薬のおかげで多くのアスリートが、もしそれがなければスポーツから引退しなければならなかったような重いけがから回復することができた」
  2)「その他の点［面］では (= in every other respect)、それを除けば」：文頭で文修飾として、また文中で語句修飾として使われる。
  - *ex.* He suffered scratches from the broken glass but was otherwise unhurt.
    「彼は割れたガラスでかすり傷を負ったが、それ以外はけがはなかった」

3）「（…とは）別なふうに、異なったやり方で（= differently, or in another way）」：than ... の比較対象を伴う場合もある。

    ex. A person is presumed innocent until proved otherwise.
    「人はそうでない（= guilty「有罪だ」）という立証があるまでは無罪の推定を受ける」
    Her personality is otherwise than I thought.
    「彼女の性格は私が思っていたのとは違った」

4　【among (many) other ...】【help の用法】

(l.45)　Since soda is unhealthy (it causes tooth problems, is linked to weight gain, and can cause diabetes, **among many other problems**), politicians believed prohibiting the sale of large quantities of soda would **help make** their city population healthier.

  ▶ among (many) other things や among others などで、「とりわけ、（他にもいろいろあるが）特に」を意味する。同類の人や物を列挙して、「…など」に近い意味のこともある。ここの among many other problems は「他にも多くの問題があるが、とりわけ…」の意味。「歯の問題を引き起こし、体重増加に関係があり、糖尿病を引き起こす可能性があるなど、数多くの問題がある」と訳してもいいだろう。

    ex. The gallery has an excellent collection of Impressionist works by, among others, Manet and Renoir.
    「その画廊には印象派の作品、とりわけマネとルノワールの素晴らしいコレクションがそろっている」
    The curriculum of the school includes math, philosophy, foreign languages, and music, among others.
    「その学校のカリキュラムには数学、哲学、外国語、音楽などが含まれている」

  ▶ 〈help+O+ (to) *do*〉で「O が〜するのを助ける」を意味するが、上記の文の help のように O がなく、〈help+ (to) *do*〉で「…するのに役立つ」を表現する形もある。help make their city population healthier で「市民をより健康にするのに役立つ」。

    ex. Moderate exercise helps prevent heart disease.「適度な運動は心臓病予防の効果がある」

The COVID-19 pandemic* has rendered the behavior of most Americans 🔊21
unrecognizable. Handshakes have turned into elbow bumps*. School and work are
conducted remotely. Socializing happens (a). And now even our faces are becoming
nearly unrecognizable as we don* a mask in order to go out.

5   Outside of an operating room or a bank robbery, masks are not the norm* in Western 🔊22
countries. At times, face coverings, whether women's veils or bandanas worn by
demonstrators, have sparked outright* bans. In some parts of the U.S. during the
pandemic, the requirement to put on a mask has brought about political protests, arrests
and even (b). A security guard in Michigan was killed after telling a customer to put
10 on a mask. Even for the large majority of Americans who are willing to follow public
health guidelines, masks have been an adjustment. They can be hot and uncomfortable.
They impede* communication and cover (1)identifying features in a way that gloves do
not. They feel, well, weird*.

But (2)weird behaviors can become standard, and long-standing customs can change, 🔊23
15 behavioral scientists say. Half a century ago the idea that dog owners should pick up
their pet's waste was so controversial that in New York City one prominent figure in the
debate had a plastic bag of droppings* thrown in her face at a public meeting. Yet
pooper-scooper* laws are now in place in cities large and small. Once upon a time, when
buying an airline ticket or booking a table at a restaurant, travelers had to choose between
20 the smoking and nonsmoking sections. Today in most of the U.S., there is no such thing
as a smoking section.

To bring about such change, a new behavior must first ascend to the status of a social 🔊24
norm. Norms include both the perception of how a group behaves and a sense of social
approval or censure* for violating that conduct. "(3)The critical thing to lock in that
25 norm is that you believe that other people expect you to do it," says behavioral economist
Syon Bhanot of Swarthmore College. That expectation already exists in places such as
hard-hit New York City, where those without masks are sometimes berated*.

The point is that masks do not just protect the wearer, they protect others. Such 🔊25
community-minded thinking fits with collectivist cultural norms in some parts of Asia,
30 where masks are routinely worn when one is sick — and where there is more experience
with serious epidemics*. Even in the more individualistic U.S., protecting others can
serve as a powerful motivator. (4)In an effort to determine what message would
encourage doctors to improve their handwashing habits, a study found that signs near
hospital sinks reminding them to protect patients by washing their hands were more
35 effective than ones reminding them to protect themselves.

Similarly, the first wave of evidence about the harms of smoking focused on damage 🔊26
to the smokers themselves and had no effect on smoking in public spaces. People

thought individuals had "the right to harm themselves," says psychologist Jay Van Bavel of New York University. "It really started to change once we realized the consequences of secondhand smoke. Do you have a right to damage kids at school, your colleagues at work or the staff at a restaurant?" So far 28 states and Washington, D.C., have said the answer is (c) and passed comprehensive smoke-free-air laws.

27   "Social norms can change rapidly," says social psychologist Catherine Sanderson of Amherst College, "and it doesn't take everybody." In (5)an online experiment conducted by researchers at the University of Pennsylvania, subjects engaged in social coordination to assign names to an object. The tipping point★ for achieving enough critical mass to initiate social change proved to be just 25 percent of participants. "They become the social influencers, the trendsetters," Sanderson says.

28   Leadership is critical, however, which is (d) behavioral scientists were so alarmed by the recent examples of Vice President Mike Pence and President Donald Trump refusing to wear masks during public appearances. "They are the primary people who are setting norms, especially when it's on television or in the news," Van Bavel says. Those politicians are flouting★ the advice of their own public health officials. In early April the Centers for Disease Control and Prevention officially recommended "wearing cloth face coverings in [A] settings where other social distancing measures are difficult to maintain." It did not help, however, that the new recommendation conflicted with earlier statements from officials suggesting that masks were ineffective or should be left for medical professionals, who needed them more.

29   The pro-mask★ message has become more consistent just a few weeks later. Multiple studies show the benefits of masks. One from statistical researchers at Arizona State University found that (6)if 80 percent of the population adopted even only moderately effective coverings, the practice would prevent as much as 45 percent of projected deaths in New York State and reduce fatality numbers by up to 65 percent in Washington State. Absent virtuous role models at the national level, state, local and private institutions, as well as celebrities, have begun to exert their considerable power to bring about change. "People are putting pictures of themselves in masks as their profile pictures," Bhanot says. Airlines and universities are requiring anyone who boards a plane or comes on campus to wear a mask. "As that gets scaled up to all elements of society, you will have greater compliance," Van Bavel says.

30   Barriers remain. The politicization★ of masks in the U.S. might mean that some areas of the country will never adopt them entirely. And endemic★ racism has led some young black men to fear that they will be mistaken for criminals if they wear masks in stores.

31   Once masks become the norm in most places, however, donning them will not seem odd or alarming, says psychologist Alexander Todorov of Princeton University, who

75 studies facial expression. "People compensate. When they meet on the street, there is more gesticulation*. People engage in strategies to make sure that they're being (e)."

In truth, the adoption of masks is happening at a surprising pace. "The vast majority 🔊 32 of people have, in a period of a few weeks, completely changed their (f) in radical ways," Van Bavel says. "In a year or three or five years, it might be more normal during 80 flu season to see Americans or people from Western Europe wear masks. This might be what changes the norm."

* pandemic「世界的流行病（の）」 bump「突き当てること」 **don**：to put on **norm**：standard
outright：complete and total **impede**：to delay or prevent someone or something by obstructing them
weird：odd, strange droppings「動物の糞（ふん）」 pooper-scooper「犬の糞をすくうシャベル」
censure：severe disapproval **berate**：to criticize angrily epidemic「流行病（の）」
tipping point「転換点、臨界点」 **flout**：to disregard openly, scorn
pro-mask：supporting the use of masks
politicization：making someone or something political in character **endemic**：deeply rooted
gesticulation：making gestures

解答欄

1 (a) .... (b) .... (c) .... (d) .... (e) .... (f) ....

2 (1) .... (3) ....

3 · ....
....
· ....
....

4 ....
....
....

5 ....
....

6 ....

7 ....
....
....

8 ....

入試基礎レベル

2　turn into ...

6　at times

8　requirement [rikwáiərmənt]

8　bring about ...

9　violence [váiələns]

11　uncomfortable [ʌnkʌ́mftəbl]

12　features [fíːtʃərz]

12　in a way that ...

16　waste [wéist]　　排せつ物

16　figure [fígjər]（名）

18　once upon a time

19　book [búk]（動）

24　lock in ...

25　expect ... to do

32　serve as ...

34　remind O to do

36　similarly [símələrli]

41　so far

46　achieve [ətʃíːv]

47　prove to be ...

49　be alarmed by ...

51　appearance [əpíərəns]

54　recommend [rèkəménd]

55　measure [méʒər]

56　maintain [meintéin]

57　statement [stéitmənt]

57　ineffective [ìniféktiv]

60　benefit [bénəfit]

62　project [prədʒékt]（動）

67　board [bɔ́ːrd]（動）

71　lead ... to do

74　alarming [əláːrmiŋ]（形）

76　make sure that ...

77　in truth

77　at a ... pace

77　vast majority

入試標準レベル（共通テスト・私大）

3　conduct [kəndʌ́kt]（動）

3　remotely [rimóutli]

5　operating room　　手術室

5　robbery [rábəri]

7　demonstrator [démənstrèitər]　デモ参加者

7　ban [bǽn]（名）

8　political protest　　政治的抗議

8　arrest [ərést]（名）

10　be willing to do

11　adjustment [ədʒʌ́stmənt]

12　identify [aidéntəfài]

18　be in place

23　perception [pərsépʃən]

24　approval [əprúːvl]

24　critical [krítikl]

26　expectation [èkspektéiʃən]

30　routinely [ruːtíːnli]

32　motivator [móutəvèitər]

32　determine [ditə́ːrmin]

36　evidence [évidəns]

38　psychologist [saikálədʒist]

39　consequence [kánsəkwèns]

40　colleague [káliːg]

45　subject [sʌ́bdʒekt]（名）

45　engage in ...

46　assign A to B

46　object [ábdʒikt]（名）

47　participant [pɑːrtísəpənt]

51　primary [práimèri]

56　recommendation [rèkəməndéiʃən]

56　conflict with ...

58　medical professional　医療専門家、医療従事者

59　consistent [kənsístənt]

60　statistical [stətístikl]

61　adopt [ədápt]

語句　音声は、「英語」→「日本語の意味」の順で読まれます。　CD 2- Tr 34-36

入試標準レベル（共通テスト・私大）

61	**moderately** [mάdərətli]	
63	**up to ...**	
64	**institution** [ìnstət(j)úːʃən]	
65	**celebrity** [səlébrəti]	
65	**considerable** [kənsídərəbl]	
70	**barrier** [bǽriər]	
71	**entirely** [intáiərli]	
72	**criminal** [kríminl]	
75	**compensate** [kάmpənsèit]	
76	**strategy** [strǽtədʒi]	
77	**adoption** [ədάpʃən]	

入試発展レベル（二次・有名私大）

1	**render A B**	
2	**unrecognizable** [ʌnrékəgnàizəbl]	
3	**virtually** [və́ːrtʃuəli]	
5	**norm**	
13	**weird** [wíərd]	奇妙な、変な
16	**controversial** [kὰntrəvə́ːrʃəl]	
16	**prominent** [prάminənt]	
22	**social norm**	
24	**violate** [váiəlèit]	
27	**hard-hit**（形）	
36	**wave of ...**	
42	**comprehensive** [kὰmprihénsiv]	
45	**coordination** [kouɔ̀ːrdənéiʃən]	
50	**Vice President**	
59	**multiple** [mʌ́ltəpl]	
64	**virtuous** [və́ːrtʃuəs]	
65	**exert** [igzə́ːrt]	
69	**compliance** [kəmpláiəns]	
71	**racism** [réisìzm]	
78	**radical** [rǽdikl]	

その他

1	**COVID-19 pandemic**	新型コロナウイルス感染症の世界的流行
3	**socialize** [sóuʃəlàiz]	人付き合いをする
6	**veil** [véil]	（顔を覆う）ベール
6	**bandana** [bændǽnə]	バンダナ
7	**spark** [spάːrk]	…を引き起こす、…の引き金となる
7	**outright** [áutràit]	完全な、徹底的な
10	**public health**	公衆衛生
11	**guideline** [gáidlàin]	指針、ガイドライン
14	**long-standing**	長年［長期］にわたる
15	**behavioral scientist**	行動科学者
17	**public meeting**	公開の会合、市民集会
22	**ascend to ...**	（地位・名声などが）…まで高まる
25	**behavioral economist**	行動経済学者
29	**community-minded**（形）	共同体志向の強い
29	**collectivist** [kəléktivist]	集産主義者（の）
31	**epidemic** [èpidémik]	（感染症などの）流行
31	**individualistic** [ìndəvìdʒuəlístik]	個人主義（者）的な
33	**handwashing** [hǽndwὰʃiŋ]	手洗い、手指消毒
40	**secondhand smoke**	副流煙
42	**smoke-free**	煙のない、禁煙の
43	**social psychologist**	社会心理学者
46	**critical mass**	必要最低限の数［量］
47	**initiate** [iníʃièit]	開始する、起こす
48	**influencer** [ínfluənsər]	影響を与える人、インフルエンサー
48	**trendsetter** [tréndsètər]	流行を作る人
53	**public health official**	公衆衛生当局者
54	**the Centers for Disease Control and Prevention**	（米国）疾病予防管理センター
55	**social distancing**	社会的距離を取ること
63	**fatality** [feitǽləti]	死亡者（数）
64	**absent** [ǽbsənt]（前）	…がなければ、…がないので
64	**role model**	他人の手本となる人物、ロールモデル
68	**get scaled up to ...**	…まで拡大される

展開	段落	要旨
主題の提示	1	COVID-19 のパンデミックは、多くのアメリカ人の（①　　　　）を変えた。
展開①	2	欧米ではマスク着用は一般的なことではない。マスクはコミュニケーションを妨げ、個人の外観を隠すので、奇妙な感じがするのだ。
展開②	3	長年の習慣が変わることもある。今では、犬の排せつ物処理を飼い主に義務づける法律があり、大半の場所で喫煙席は存在しなくなった。
展開③	4	変化するためには新しい行動を（②　　　　）にする必要がある。重要な要素は、そのように行動することを他人から期待されている、と信じるようになることだ。
展開④	5	マスク着用が（③　　　　）も守るという点が重要だ。個人主義的なアメリカでも、（③　　　　）を守ることは強力な動機づけとなる。
展開⑤	6	喫煙者自身への害に関する証拠は、公共の場での喫煙に影響を与えなかった。しかし、副流煙の影響が認識されたことで、受動喫煙防止法が制定された。
展開⑥	7	ある研究によれば、社会的規範の変化は参加者のわずか（④　　　　）が変わることで起こる。
展開⑦	8	規範作りにはリーダーシップが重要だが、大統領らは公衆衛生当局の忠告を無視してマスク着用を拒否した。当局の声明に（⑤　　　　）があったことも、事態をさらに悪化させた。
展開⑧	9	後にマスク推奨のメッセージは一貫したものになった。変化を起こそうと地方自治体や有名人などが行動したため、マスク着用はさらに順守されるようになるだろう。
展開⑨	10	障壁は政治的問題と、マスク着用で（⑥　　　　）と間違われることへの黒人の恐れなどだ。
展開⑩	11	しかし、マスクが規範になれば、マスクは奇妙なものには見えなくなるだろう。
結論	12	マスクの採用は驚異的速さで進んだ。欧米人の規範が変わるかもしれない。

（下書き）

10　　　　　　　　　　　　　　　　　　20

10　　　　　　　　　　　　　　　　　　20

本文解説

1 【同格節を導く that】【so ～ that ...】【have ＋ O ＋過去分詞】

(l.15) Half a century ago **the idea that** dog owners should pick up their pet's waste was **so** controversial **that** in New York City one prominent figure in the debate **had** a plastic bag of droppings **thrown** in her face at a public meeting.

- ▶ the idea that dog ... waste が全体の主部で、that 節は名詞 the idea の内容を説明する〈同格〉の名詞節。「犬の飼い主は…すべきだという考え」の意味。
- ▶ so controversial that in ... debate は〈so ～ that ...〉の構文で、「とても～なので…だ」の意味。
- ▶ had a plastic bag of droppings thrown は〈have ＋ O ＋過去分詞〉「O を～される」の形で、「糞の入ったポリ袋を投げつけられた」の意味。a plastic bag of droppings was thrown という受動の意味であることに注意。同じ〈have ＋ O ＋過去分詞〉の形で「O を～してもらう」の意味になることもある。文脈で判断しよう。
  - *ex.* He had his bicycle stolen and had to walk back to his house.
    「自転車を盗まれ、彼は家まで歩いて帰らなければならなかった」
    She has her teeth checked every month.「彼女は毎月歯を検査してもらっている」

2 【there is no such thing as ...】

(l.20) Today in most of the U.S., **there is no such thing as** a smoking section.

- ▶ there is no such thing as ... で「…のようなものはない、…なんて存在しない」という定型表現。such a thing のように a はつかないので注意。"something does not exist or is not possible" を強調して使われる。人については there is no such person as ...「…のような人は存在しない」となる。他に、no such luck「残念［だめ］だった、ついてなかった」などの表現がある。
  - *ex.* There's no such thing as a free lunch.「ただ（の食事）ほど高い［怖い］ものはない」
    I expected my father would pick me up at the station, but (I had) no such luck.
    「父が駅で車に乗せてくれるかと期待したけど、残念、それはなかった」

3 【関係副詞 where の用法】

(l.26) That expectation already exists in places such as hard-hit New York City, **where** those without masks are sometimes berated.

(l.28) Such community-minded thinking fits with collectivist cultural norms in some parts of Asia, **where** masks are routinely worn when one is sick — and **where** there is more experience with serious epidemics.

- ▶ 関係副詞の where は場所を表す先行詞を修飾する。第 1 文の where は places such as hard-hit New York City を先行詞とする関係副詞で、その前にコンマが置かれた非制限用法［継続用法］。where 以下でその場所について追加の説明を加える用法で、「そして、そうした場所では…だ」のように訳せる。先行詞が固有名詞の場合、非制限用法が普通である。
- ▶ 第 2 文には 2 つの where があるが、どちらも some parts of Asia を先行詞とする非制限用法［継続用法］の関係副詞。アジアの一部地域について追加の説明を加えている。

4 【the point is that ...】【not just ～ , (but also) ...】

(l.28) **The point is that** masks do **not just** protect the wearer, they protect others.

- ▶ the point is that ... で「大切なことは［要点は］…である」。that 以下は is の補語の働きをする名詞節。
- ▶ not just A but (also) B は not only A but (also) B と同じく「A だけでなく B も」を表すが、ここでは but also が省略され、コンマによって結ばれる形になっている。全体で「大切なことは、マスクが着用者を守るだけでなく、他者をも守るということである」。
  - *ex.* The point is to start work right away.「重要なのは、すぐ仕事にとりかかることだ」
    Learning a foreign language requires not just hard work, but courage as well.
    「外国語を学ぶには、勤勉さだけではなく勇気も必要だ」

5 【subject, object】

(l.44) In an online experiment conducted by researchers at the University of Pennsylvania, **subjects** engaged in social coordination to assign names to an **object**.

▶ subject は多義語だが、ここでは「（実験などの）被験者（= a person or thing being used to study something, especially in an experiment)」。実験や研究に関する文脈で頻出する。object も同様に多義語で、ここではその subjects が取り組んだ実験「ある物に名前をつける社会的協調活動」の「物」を意味する。

▶ subject には名詞、形容詞、動詞の用法、object には名詞、動詞の用法がある。以下、それぞれの文脈での意味を辞書等で確かめてみよう。

subject : "What was your favorite subject in school?"
"This conversation is unpleasant. Let's change the subject."
"My grandma's poor health makes her subject to colds."
object : "The object of the game is to get to know each other."
"My father objected to my working part-time."

6 【it did not help that ...】

(l.53) In early April the Centers for Disease Control and Prevention officially recommended "wearing cloth face coverings in … ." **It did not help**, however, **that** the new recommendation conflicted with earlier statements from officials suggesting that masks were ineffective or should be left for medical professionals, who needed them more.

▶ help はここでは自動詞で、「助けになる、役立つ」の意味。全体の直訳は「しかし、that 以下のことは役立たなかった」だが、〈It did not help that ~〉は、その文の前に書かれた内容や状況を受けて、「~によってさらに悪化した」といった意味を表す。一種の「修辞表現」で、皮肉を込めた場合が多い。以下の native speaker のコメントを参照。

▶ The phrase "it did not help that A" is used sarcastically to mean that A actually made the situation worse. The literal meaning of the words does not indicate this, but the phrase is now commonly used and understood in the more negative sense. The sentence in the passage could be rewritten as: "The new recommendation conflicted with earlier statements from officials suggesting that masks were ineffective or should be left for medical professionals, who needed them more. These conflicting messages increased the level of distrust of public health authorities by some Americans, who then chose to ignore masking recommendations."

7 【in の用法】

(l.79) "**In** a year or three or five years, it might be more normal during flu season to see Americans or people from Western Europe wear masks."

▶ in a year ... の in は、現在を基準に時間の経過を表して「…後に、…たって、…のうちに」の意味を表す。通例未来表現とともに使われる。ここでは might が使われ、未来の可能性を推量している。
ex. I'll be back in two hours.「2 時間したら戻ります」

▶ 上記に似た用法で、必要期間などを表して「…の間に［で］」を意味する in の用法もある。
ex. This problem is super easy. You can solve it in ten minutes.
「この問題は超簡単だよ。君なら 10 分で解けるよ」

Computer programs have reached a difficult point in their long journey toward ⊘37
artificial intelligence (AI). They surpass people at tasks such as playing poker or
recognizing faces in a crowd. Meanwhile, self-driving cars using similar technology run
into pedestrians and posts and we wonder whether they can ever be reliable.

⁵ Among (1)these rapid developments and continuing problems, one essential building
block of human intelligence has proven difficult for machines for decades: Understanding
cause and effect.

Put simply, today's machine-learning programs can't tell whether a crowing chicken ⊘38
makes the sun rise, or the other way around. Whatever volumes of data a machine
¹⁰ analyzes, it cannot understand what a human gets intuitively. From the time we are
infants, we organize our experiences into causes and effects. (2)The questions "Why did
this happen?" and "What if I had acted differently?" are what make us human, and so
far are missing from machines.

Suppose, for example, that a drugstore decides to leave its pricing to a machine-learning ⊘39
¹⁵ program that we'll call Charlie. The program reviews the store's records and sees that
past variations of the price of toothpaste haven't correlated with changes in sales volume.
So Charlie recommends raising the price to generate more revenue. A month later, the
sales of toothpaste have dropped — along with dental floss, cookies and other items.
(3)Where did Charlie go wrong?

²⁰ Charlie didn't understand that the previous (human) manager varied prices only ⊘40
when the competing stores did. When Charlie one-sidedly raised the price, price-conscious
customers took their business elsewhere. The example shows that historical data alone
tells us nothing about causes — and that the direction of causation is crucial.

Machine-learning systems have made surprising progress at analyzing data patterns,
²⁵ but that is the low-hanging fruit of AI. To reach the higher fruit, AI needs a ladder, which
we call the Ladder of Causation. Its steps represent three levels of reasoning.

The first step is Association, the level for current machines and many animals; on that ⊘41
step, Pavlov's dogs learned to associate a bell with food. The next is Intervention: What
will happen if I ring a bell, or raise the price of toothpaste? Intervention is different from
³⁰ observation; raising the price one-sidedly is different from seeing what happened in the
past. The highest step is (4)Counterfactual, which means the ability to imagine results,
reflect on one's actions and assess other scenarios. Imagine giving a self-driving car this

ability.　After an accident, its CPU would ask itself questions like: What would have happened if I had not honked at the drunken pedestrian?

✎42　To reach the higher steps, machines need a model of the causal factors — essentially, ³⁵ a mathematics of cause and effect.　A simple element might be: "Liquor affects people's judgment, and that makes them move in unexpected ways."　We can describe this using what scientists now call a causal diagram, in which arrows represent a series of possible causes: (5)Liquor ≫ Affected Judgment ≫ Unexpected Motion.　Such diagrams enable the car to predict that certain pedestrians will react differently to the honking of its horn. ⁴⁰ They also give us the possibility of "interrogating" the car to explain its process: Why did you honk your horn?

✎43　Current machine-learning systems can reach higher steps only in areas where the rules are not violated, such as playing chess.　Outside those areas, they are fragile and easily make mistakes.　But with causal models, a machine can predict the results of ⁴⁵ actions that haven't been tried before, reflect on its actions, and apply its learned skills to new situations.

1

2

3

4

5

6

7

| 語句 | 音声は、「英語」→「日本語の意味」の順で読まれます。 | CD 2- Tr 44-47 |

入試基礎レベル

11 **organize** [ɔ́:rgənàiz] ....

12 **so far** ....

17 **recommend** [rèkəménd] ....

18 **item** [áitəm] ....

20 **manager** [mǽnidʒər] ....

20 **vary** [véəri] ....

25 **ladder** [lǽdər] ....

35 **factor** [fǽktər] ....

35 **essentially** [isénʃəli] ....

46 **apply A to B** ....

入試標準レベル（共通テスト・私大）

2 **artificial intelligence (AI)** ....

3 **meanwhile** [mí:nhwàil]（副）.....................

3 **run into ...** ....

4 **post** [póust]（名）　柱、支柱、くい

4 **reliable** [riláiəbl] ....

7 **cause and effect** ....

8 **put simply** ....

11 **infant** [ínfənt] ....

12 **What if 〜?** ....

13 **missing** [mísiŋ]（形）.....................

14 **Suppose that 〜.** ....

15 **review** [rivjú:]（動）.....................

17 **generate** [dʒénərèit] ....

20 **previous** [prí:viəs] ....

21 **competing** [kəmpí:tiŋ]（形）.....................

23 **crucial** [krú:ʃəl] ....

26 **represent** [rèprizént] ....

27 **association** [əsòusiéiʃən] ....

28 **associate A with B** ....

30 **observation** [àbzərvéiʃən] ....

34 **drunken** [drʌ́ŋkən]（形）.....................

36 **liquor** [líkər] ....

38 **diagram** [dáiəgræm] ....

38 **a series of ...** ....

40 **react to ...** ....

40 **horn** [hɔ́:rn] ....

入試発展レベル（二次・有名私大）

2 **surpass** [sərpǽs] ....

3 **self-driving car** ....

4 **pedestrian** [pədéstriən] ....

9 **the other way around** ....

16 **variation** [vèəriéiʃən] ....

16 **sales volume** ....

26 **reasoning** [rí:zəniŋ]（名）.....................

28 **intervention** [intərvénʃən] ....

32 **reflect on ...** ....

32 **assess** [əsés] ....

32 **scenario** [sənǽriòu] ....

37 **unexpected** [ʌ̀nikspéktid]（形）.....................

44 **violate** [váiəlèit] ....

44 **fragile** [frǽdʒəl] ....

その他

2 **poker** [póukər]　ポーカー

5 **building block**　構成要素、基本的要素

8 **machine-learning program**　機械学習プログラム

8 **crow** [króu]（動）　（おんどりが）鳴く

10 **intuitively** [intú:ətivli]　直感的に

14 **pricing** [práisiŋ]（名）　価格決定［設定］

16 **toothpaste** [tú:θpèist]　歯磨き粉

16 **correlate with ...**　…と相関する

17 **revenue** [révənjù:]　収益、収入

18 **dental floss**　デンタルフロス、糸式ようじ

21 **one-sidedly**　一方的に

21 **price-conscious**　価格に敏感な

22 **take *one's* business elsewhere**　他の店に行って買い物をする

23 **causation** [kɔːzéiʃən]　因果関係

25 **low-hanging fruit**　簡単に達成できる目標

31 **counterfactual** [kàuntərfǽktʃuəl]（名）　反事実（的思考）

34 **honk** [hɑ́ŋk]（動）　（クラクションを）鳴らす

35 **causal** [kɔ́:zəl]（形）　因果関係を示す

41 **interrogate** [intérəgèit]　尋問する

展開	段落	要旨
主題の提示	1	コンピュータープログラムは高度に発達したが、まだ問題も多く、（①　　　　　　　）開発において困難な地点にいる。
主題の展開①	2	人間の（②　　　　　　）に不可欠な原因と結果の理解が、機械には難しいことが判明している。
主題の展開②	3	機械は人間と違い、（③　　　　　　　　）を分析しても、体験を因果関係に整理することができない。
主題の展開③	4	あるプログラムは、過去のデータから価格変動と（④　　　　　　）に相関がないと判断し、商品の値上げをしたが、売上は減少した。
主題の展開④	5	プログラムの失敗例は、因果関係の（⑤　　　　　　）が重要であることを示している。
主題の展開⑤	6	械機械学習システムがより高い成果を得るには、「（⑥　　　　　　　　　　　　）」が必要だ。
主題の展開⑥	7	（⑥　　　　　　　　　　）は、「連想」、「（⑦　　　　　　）」、「反事実（的思考）」の３段階から成る。
主題の展開⑦	8	機械が高度な段階に到達するには、因果要因のモデルが必要となる。これにより、機械は結果の（⑧　　　　　　）や判断過程の説明が可能となる。
結論	9	現在の機械学習システムは、限定的な分野でのみ高度な段階に到達できる。因果関係モデルを使えば、前例のない行動結果の（⑧　　　　　　）や行動の検討、学習したスキルの応用が可能となるだろう。

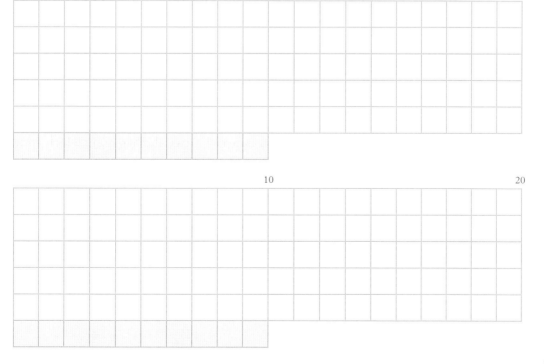

（下書き）　　　　　　　　　　　　　　　　　　10　　　　　　　　　　　　　　　　　20

10　　　　　　　　　　　　　　　　　20

本文解説

1 【put simply】【the other way around】

(l.8) **Put simply**, today's machine-learning programs can't tell whether a crowing chicken makes the sun rise, or **the other way around**.

> ▶ put simply は通例文頭に置いて、「簡単に言えば」。to put it simply, simply put とも言う。この put は「（考え・気持ちなどを）述べる、言い表す（= express; say or write something using words in a particular way）」の意味で、応用範囲が広い。
> > *ex.* That man is selfish and rude. To put it mildly, I don't like him at all.
> > 「あの男は身勝手で無礼だ。控えめに言うと、全く好きじゃない」

> ▶ the other way around[round] で「逆に、あべこべに（= the opposite of what you have just mentioned）」。しばしば前に or, not, instead of, rather than などを伴って使われる。この文では直前の a crowing chicken makes the sun rise に対して、因果関係が逆の the rising sun makes a chicken crow あるいは a chicken crows in response to the sunrise といった意味。
> > *ex.* The Earth moves around the Sun, not the other way around.
> > 「地球が太陽の周りを回っているのであって、その逆ではない」

2 【複合関係詞 whatever】【volumes of ...】

(l.9) **Whatever volumes of data a machine analyzes**, it cannot understand what a human gets intuitively.

> ▶ whatever は関係代名詞 what に -ever がついた複合関係詞と呼ばれるもので、ここでは直後に名詞句を置いて形容詞的に使われている。この文では副詞節を導いて、「たとえどんな〜でも」という〈譲歩〉の意味を表している。volumes of ... は「大量の…、多くの…」。全体で「機械はたとえどんなに多量のデータを分析しても」の意味。No matter what volumes of data a machine analyzes とも表現できる。
> > *ex.* Whatever difficulties you have, I'm sure you'll be able to overcome them.
> > 「どんな困難に遭おうと、君はきっとそれを克服できると思う」

3 【we'll call vs. we call】

(l.14) Suppose, for example, that a drugstore decides to leave its pricing to a machine-learning program that **we'll call** Charlie.

(l.25) To reach the higher fruit, AI needs a ladder, which **we call** the Ladder of Causation.

(l.37) We can describe this using what **scientists now call** a causal diagram, in which arrows represent a series of possible causes: Liquor ≫ Affected Judgment ≫ Unexpected Motion.

> ▶ we'll call Charlie の 'll = will は、一人称（I, we）の主語が、あらかじめ考えたことではなく、その場で決めた意志や意図を表す用法。「あるドラッグストアが価格設定を機械学習プログラム、ここでは仮にチャーリーと呼ぶことにするが、そのチャーリーに任せることを決定したとしよう」の意味。
> > *ex.* "There's no laundry detergent." "OK, I'll get some."
> > 「洗濯用の洗剤がないよ」「わかった。買いに行ってくるよ。」

> ▶ we'll call ... に対し a ladder, which we call ... と what scientists now call ... には現在形の call が使われている。それぞれ「はしごが AI には必要だが、我々はそれを…と呼んでいる」、「科学者が…と呼んでいるもの」の意味で、現在の事実を述べている。

(l.21)　When Charlie one-sidedly raised the price, price-conscious customers **took their business elsewhere**.

> ▶ take *one's* business elsewhere は「仕事をよそに回す、（客が）他の店に行って買い物をする（= to go to another place to do business; to switch to another business for *one's* dealings）」の意味。「価格に敏感な顧客はチャーリーの店を敬遠して、他の店に行って購入した」ということ。
>
>　　*ex.* The angry customer said he would take his business elsewhere.
>
>　　「怒った客は、他の店に行くぞと言った」

(l.24)　Machine-learning systems have made surprising progress at analyzing data patterns, but that is the **low-hanging fruit** of AI.

> ▶ low-hanging fruit「低いところにぶら下がっている果実」は、木に登らず、地面に立って手を伸ばせばすぐもぎ取れることから、比喩的に「（大きな努力をしなくても）簡単に達成できる目標［課題・仕事］（= a job that is easy to do, or something that is very easy to achieve）」という意味で使われる。

CD 2

Social networks often stand accused of being enemies of productivity. According to 🔊48
one popular (if questionable) online source of information, the use of Facebook, Twitter
and other such sites at work costs the American economy $650 billion each year. Our
attention spans are weakening, our test scores declining, because of these "weapons of
5 mass distraction." Yet (1)such worries have arisen before. In England in the late 1600s,
similar concerns were expressed about another new media-sharing environment, the
appeal of which seemed to be undermining young people's ability to concentrate on their
studies and their work: the coffeehouse. It was the social-networking site of its day.

Like coffee itself, coffeehouses were an import from the Arab world. England's first 🔊49
10 coffeehouse opened in Oxford in the early 1650s, and hundreds of similar establishments
sprang up across England in the following years. People went to coffeehouses not just
to drink coffee, but to read the latest pamphlets and news-sheets, catch up on rumor and
gossip, and talk to other coffee drinkers, both friends and strangers. Some coffeehouses
were used as post offices, and (A)patrons would visit their favorite coffeehouses several
15 times a day to check for mail. Some coffeehouses specialized in discussion of particular
topics, like politics, literature or business. As customers moved from one shop to another,
information circulated with them in wide-ranging conversations. (2)One reason these
conversations were so lively was that social distinctions were not recognized within
coffeehouse walls. Patrons were not merely permitted but encouraged to strike up
20 conversations with strangers from entirely different walks of life.

Not everyone was pleased. Critics worried that coffeehouses were keeping people 🔊50
from productive work. But rather than functioning as enemies of industry, coffeehouses
were in fact hotbeds of creativity because of the way in which they facilitated the mixing
of both people and ideas. Members of the Royal Society, England's pioneering scientific
25 society, frequently retired to coffeehouses to extend their discussions. It was a coffeehouse
argument among fellow scientists that spurred Isaac Newton to write his foundational
works of modern science.

Coffeehouses were platforms for innovation in the world of business, too. Merchants 🔊51
used coffeehouses as meeting rooms, which gave rise to new companies and business
30 models. A London coffeehouse called Jonathan's, where merchants kept particular tables
to transact business, turned into the London Stock Exchange. Lloyd's coffeehouse, a
popular meeting place for ship captains, ship-owners and traders, became the well-
known insurance market. And the economist Adam Smith wrote much of his masterpiece
The Wealth of Nations in the British Coffee House, a popular meeting place for Scottish
35 intellectuals, among whom he circulated early drafts of his book for discussion.

52 [a] there was some time-wasting going on in coffeehouses. But their merits far outweighed their drawbacks. (3)<u>Now the spirit of the coffeehouse has been reborn in our social-media platforms.</u> They, too, are open to all comers, and allow people from different walks of life to meet, debate, and share information with friends and strangers alike, making new connections and sparking new ideas. Such conversations may be entirely 40 virtual, but they have enormous potential to bring about change in the real world. Progressive companies are embracing "enterprise social networks" to encourage collaboration, discover hidden talents and knowledge among their employees, and reduce the use of e-mail. A recent study found that use of social networking within companies increased productivity by 20 to 25 percent. The use of social media in education, 45 meanwhile, demonstrates that students learn more effectively when they interact with other learners. There is always an adjustment period when new technologies appear. During this transitional phase, which can take years, technologies are often criticized for disrupting existing ways of doing things. But what we understand from the coffeehouse is that modern fears about the dangers of social networking are (B)<u>overdone</u>. As we 50 grapple with the issues raised by new technologies, there is much we can learn from the past.

解答欄

1 (1) ....

....

(2) ....

....

2 ....

....

3 (1) ....

....

(2) ....

....

4 ....

....

....

5 (A) .... (B) ....

6 (1) .... (2) .... (3) .... (4) ....

入試基礎レベル

7　**appeal** [əpíːl]（名）

7　**concentrate on ...**

43　**employee** [èmplɔí:]

入試標準レベル（共通テスト・私大）

1　**(be) accused of ...**

1　**productivity** [pròudʌktívəti]

2　**questionable** [kwéstʃənəbl]

10　**establishment** [estǽbliʃmənt]

15　**specialize in ...**

17　**wide-ranging**（形）

18　**distinction** [distínkʃən]

23　**creativity** [krìːeitívəti]

26　**fellow** [félou]

28　**merchant** [mə́ːrtʃənt]

29　**give rise to ...**

33　**economist** [ikánəmist]

35　**intellectual** [ìntəléktʃuəl]（名）

42　**progressive** [prəgrésiv]

43　**hidden** [hídn]（形）

46　**demonstrate** [démənstrèit]

48　**(be) criticized for ...**

入試発展レベル（二次・有名私大）

5　**distraction** [distrǽkʃən]

5　**arise** [əráiz]

7　**undermine** [ʌ̀ndərmáin]

11　**spring up**

17　**circulate** [sə́ːrkjəlèit]（自動詞）

19　**not merely A but (also) B**

20　**walk of life**

21　**critic** [krítik]

23　**facilitate** [fəsílətèit]

24　**pioneering** [pàiəníəriŋ]（形）

26　**spur ... to** *do*

28　**platform** [plǽtfɔ̀ːrm]

28　**innovation** [ìnəvéiʃən]

31　**transact** [trænsǽkt]

32　**trader** [tréidər]

33　**masterpiece** [mǽstərpìːs]

35　**circulate** [sə́ːrkjəlèit]（他動詞）

35　**draft** [drǽft]

36　**time-wasting**（名）

37　**reborn** [ribɔ́ːrn]（形）

41　**virtual** [və́ːrtʃuəl]

42　**embrace** [embréis]

43　**collaboration** [kəlæ̀bəréiʃən]

46　**interact with ...**

49　**disrupt** [disrʌ́pt]

その他

1　**stand** [stǽnd]　…の状態である

4　**attention span**　集中力が持続する時間

6　**media-sharing**（形）　メディアを共有する

12　**news-sheet**　会報、公報、1枚新聞

14　**patron** [péitrən]　常連、お得意客、顧客

19　**strike up a conversation**　会話を始める

23　**hotbed of ...**　…の温床

24　**the Royal Society**　（英国）王立協会

26　**foundational** [faundéiʃənəl]
　　基礎を成す、土台となる

31　**London Stock Exchange**
　　ロンドン証券取引所

34　*The Wealth of Nations*
　　『国富論』

37　**outweigh** [àutwéi]　より上回る、勝る

37　**drawback** [drɔ́ːbæ̀k]　欠点、難点

40　**spark a new idea**
　　新たなアイディアを生み出す

42　**enterprise social network**
　　企業内ソーシャルネットワーク

47　**adjustment period**　調整期間、順応期間

48　**transitional phase**　移行期間、過渡期

50　**overdone** [òuvərdʌ́n]（形）　過剰の、大げさな

51　**grapple with ...**　…に取り組む、立ち向かう

展開	段落	要旨
本論①	1	（①　　　　　　　　　　　　　　）は生産性の敵だとしばしば非難される。だが、17 世紀の英国でも、（②　　　　　　　　　　　）に対して同様の懸念が示されたことがある。
本論②	2	（②　　　　　　　　　　　）では、職業や階級を超えて、誰でも情報交換することが奨励されていた。
本論③	3	（②　　　　　　　　　　　）は生産性を妨げると懸念する人もいたが、実際は（③　　　　　　　　）を生み出す場として機能した。
本論④	4	（②　　　　　　　　　　　）における議論は（④　　　　　　　　　　）における革新ももたらした。
結論	5	（②　　　　　　　　　　　）の利点は欠点をはるかにしのぐもので、その精神は（⑤　　　　　　　　　　　　）の討論の場によみがえっている。（②　　　　　　　　　　）の例を考えれば、（①　　　　　　　　　　　　　　）への現在の懸念は過剰だとわかる。

（下書き）

本文解説

1 【stand の用法】【accuse A of B】

(l. 1) Social networks often **stand accused of** being enemies of productivity.

▶ 〈stand ＋形容詞 / 過去分詞〉で「…の状態にある、…のままである」の意味を表す。この stand は be 動詞で言い換え可能なことが多い。stand accused of being ... は「…であると非難されている」。

ex. The back gate stood open so they slipped in through it.
「裏門が開いていたので、彼らはそこから忍び込んだ」

▶ accuse A of B「A を B のことで非難する、訴える」。People often accuse social networks of being enemies of productivity. → Social networks are often accused of being enemies of productivity. 上記の文ではこの are の代わりに stand が使われている。

ex. She has been accused of stealing her colleague's ideas and publishing them.
「彼女は同僚のアイディアを盗用しそれを発表した、と訴えられている」

2 【"weapons of mass distraction"】

(l. 3) Our attention spans are weakening, our test scores declining, because of these **"weapons of mass distraction."**

▶ these "weapons of mass distraction" とは、前の 2 文に述べられている Facebook, Twitter などの social networks を指す。

▶ "weapons of mass distraction" は、weapons of mass destruction「大量破壊兵器」という決まった表現を下敷きにした「言葉遊び」とも言うべきもので、引用符 (quotation marks) に挟まれているのもそのためである。distraction [distrǽkʃən]（「気を散らすもの、娯楽」）と destruction [distrʌ́kʃən]（「破壊」）の 2 語が発音が大変似ていることに加えて、social networks は「集中力とテストの点数を落とす」ような「気を散らすもの」であると同時に、学力を「破壊するもの」でもあるという、意味的にも見事な「掛詞」になっている。ちなみに、*Weapons of Mass Distraction* (1997) というタイトルの映画があったので、それも下敷きにしているのかもしれない。

3 【名詞＋ of which ...】【文構造】

(l. 5) In England in the late 1600s, similar concerns were expressed about another new media-sharing environment, **the appeal of which** seemed to be undermining young people's ability to concentrate on their studies and their work: the coffeehouse.

▶ which の先行詞は another new media-sharing environment で、コンマを挟んで使われている非制限用法である。of which は which の所有格で、the appeal of which は whose appeal とも表現できる。

▶ the appeal of which 以下は another new media-sharing environment「別の新たなメディアを共有する環境」の説明だが、its appeal(= the appeal of another new media-sharing environment) seemed to be undermining young people's ability to concentrate on their studies and their work「その魅力によって若者たちの学業や仕事への集中力が損なわれているように思われた」と、similar concerns「同様の懸念」の具体的な内容にもなっている。最後に another new media-sharing environment とは the coffeehouse だったと明かされる。

4　【not just A but (also) B】【not merely A but (also) B】

(l.11)　People went to coffeehouses **not just to drink coffee**, **but to read** the latest pamphlets and news-sheets, catch up on rumor and gossip, and talk to other coffee drinkers, both friends and strangers.

(l.19)　Patrons were **not merely permitted but encouraged** to strike up conversations with strangers from entirely different walks of life.

> ▶ 〈not just A but (also) B〉と〈not merely A but (also) B〉はどちらも「A だけでなく B も」の意味を表す。〈not only A but (also) B〉と同意。
> ▶ 2 つ目の文では、not permitted も to strike up conversations with strangers from entirely different walks of life に続くことに注意。「常連客は、まったく異なる職業、階級の見知らぬ人々との会話を単に許されていただけではなく、そうすることを奨励されていた」

5　【rather than ...】【the way in which ...】

(l.22)　But **rather than** functioning as enemies of industry, coffeehouses were in fact hotbeds of creativity because of **the way in which** they facilitated the mixing of both people and ideas.

> ▶ rather than ... は「…よりはむしろ、…どころか」。動名詞 functioning の意味上の主語は coffeehouses なので、「コーヒーハウスは、産業の敵として作用するどころか、〜だった」。
> ▶ in which の which の先行詞は the way。「〜する方法」には the way that [in which] 〜が使われるが、that [in which] が省略されることも多い。the way how 〜は不可。
> *ex.*　He dislikes the way (in which) young people talk. 「彼は若者たちの話し方が気に入らない」
> ▶ hotbed: a place where a lot of a particular type of activity, especially bad or violent activity, happens　ここでは「創造性を生み出す場」と肯定的な意味に使われている。 facilitate: make it easier for a process or activity to happen

6　【同格】【among whom ...】

(l.33)　And **the economist Adam Smith** wrote much of **his masterpiece *The Wealth of Nations*** in **the British Coffee House**, **a popular meeting place for Scottish intellectuals**, **among whom** he circulated early drafts of his book for discussion.

> ▶ the economist と Adam Smith、his masterpiece と *The Wealth of Nations* は同格、the British Coffee House と a popular meeting place for Scottish intellectuals も同格。
> ▶ among whom の whom の先行詞は Scottish intellectuals で、among 以下は and he(= Adam Smith) circulated early drafts of his book among them (= Scottish intellectuals) for discussion の意味。

Growing evidence that countries where there is more inequality of income are places where there is less equality of opportunity helps us understand why the United States has become one of the advanced countries with the least equality of opportunity. A young American's life prospects are more dependent on the income and education of his parents than those of young people in other advanced nations.

Inequities in access to education are among the reasons the United States is no longer the land of opportunity. Even more disastrous is how education perpetuates advantages and disadvantages: of Americans born around 1980, only about 9 percent of those from the bottom quarter of the income distribution graduated from college. One reason for (1)this is the cost of higher education.

And in the United States, "justice for all" is supposed to be its slogan. Yet increasingly, America is more appropriately described as offering "justice for those who can afford it." The rule of law is supposed to protect the weak against the strong. And it is supposed to mean that the law is (2)impartially enforced. We have laws that are designed to protect people from unjust takings of their property. But we didn't enforce the laws against the bankers — not a single one went to jail for the gross miscarriage of justice★ in the financial crisis of 2008.

Earlier I described America's high level of inequality of opportunity. A large fraction of Americans — those that weren't lucky enough to be born of parents of means — have little chance of living up to their potential. (3)This is, of course, a disaster for these individuals, but it is also bad for the economy: we are not using fully our most important resource, our people.

As a government of the 1 percent, for the 1 percent, and by the 1 percent works to enrich the 1 percent, through welfare and tax benefits, fewer resources are available for investments in infrastructure, education, and technology, investments that are needed to keep the economy strong and growing.

But the real cost of inequality is to our democracy and our society. Basic values for which the country has stood — equality of opportunity, equal access to justice, a sense of a system that is fair — have been eroded. A tax system such as ours is, for instance, based on voluntary compliance. It works if there is a belief that the system is fair — but (4)it is now evident to all that ours is not, that those at the top get a far better deal than those in the middle.

61   As in so many other instances, when troubles emerged, the financial sector demanded to be paid back first — putting the welfare of ordinary citizens, including workers with contracts promising them retirement benefits, (5)<u>in the backseat</u>.

35

No society can function without trust. Although economists typically don't use words like "trust," in fact, our economy simply can't function without trust. And inequality has eroded this most precious thing, and (6)<u>once eroded, it may be hard to restore</u>.

   ★ miscarriage of justice「誤審」

解答欄

1
....
....

2
....

3
....
....

4
....
....

5
....

6
....
....

7
....

語句 音声は、「英語」→「日本語の意味」の順で読まれます。 CD 2- Tr 62-65

入試基礎レベル

1 growing [gróuiŋ] (形)

1 income [ínkʌm]

2 opportunity [àpərtúːnəti]

3 advanced country

6 no longer ...

11 be supposed to *do*

12 describe A as B

13 afford [əfɔ́ːrd]

13 protect A against[from] B

15 property [prápərti]

21 disaster [dizǽstər]

22 resource [ríːsɔ̀ːrs] (名)

24 be available for ...

34 including ... (前)

36 function [fʌ́ŋkʃən] (動)

入試標準レベル（共通テスト・私大）

1 evidence [évid(e)ns]

4 prospect [práspekt] (名)

11 justice [dʒʌ́stis]

12 increasingly

12 appropriately [əpróupriətli]

15 be designed to *do*

16 not a single ...

19 be born of ...

20 have little chance of ...

20 potential [pəténʃəl] (名)

24 welfare [wélfèər]

25 investment [invéstmənt]

28 stand for ...

33 emerge [imɔ́ːrdʒ]

35 contract [kántrækt] (名)

35 retirement [ritáiərmənt]

36 economist [ikánəmist]

36 typically [típikəli]

37 simply ... not

38 precious [préʃəs]

39 restore [ristɔ́ːr]

入試発展レベル（二次・有名私大）

1 inequality [ìnikwáləti]

7 disastrous [dizǽstrəs]

7 perpetuate [pərpétʃuèit]

11 slogan [slóugn]

14 enforce [enfɔ́ːrs]

15 unjust [ʌndʒʌ́st]

16 go to jail

17 gross [gróus] (形)

17 financial crisis

20 means [míːnz]

24 enrich [enrítʃ]

25 infrastructure [ínfrəstrʌ̀ktʃər]

29 erode [iróud]

30 voluntary [váləntèri]

30 compliance [kəmpláiəns]

その他

6 access to education 教育の機会

9 income distribution 所得分布

13 rule of law 法の支配、法治

14 impartially [impáːrʃəli] 偏らずに、公平に

18 a large fraction of ... …の大部分、大多数

20 live up to ... …に沿う、応えて生きる

24 benefits 給付金、手当

28 access to justice 司法制度の利用

31 get a good deal よい待遇を受ける

33 financial sector 金融部門

35 backseat [bǽksìt] 重要でない地位、二の次

各段落のまとめとなるように、空所に適切な語句を入れなさい。（同じ番号には、同じ語句が入ります）

展開	段落	要旨
主題の提示	1	米国は機会の（①　　　　　　　）が最も少ない先進国の1つだ。若者の人生の可能性は、親の（②　　　　　　　）と学歴に強く依存している。
主題の展開①	2	（③　　　　　　　）の機会の不平等は、米国の機会の不平等の理由の1つであり、高額な高等（③　　　　　　　）が有利不利を永続化させている。
主題の展開②	3	米国はますます「金持ちのための（④　　　　　　　）」を提供している。
主題の展開③	4	経済力のない家庭の子が（⑤　　　　　　　）を発揮する機会は少なく、それは経済全体にとってもマイナスである。
主題の展開④	5	（②　　　　　　　）の多い者を豊かにする制度によって、経済成長に必要な（⑥　　　　　　　）が制限されている。
主題の展開⑤	6	不平等のコストを真に背負うのは（⑦　　　　　　　）と社会である。制度が公正であるという基本的な価値観はむしばまれてしまっている。
主題の展開⑥	7	問題が発生すると、金融部門はまず返済を求め、一般市民の（⑧　　　　　　　）を二の次にした。
主題の展開⑦	8	社会に不可欠な「（⑨　　　　　　　）」を不平等がむしばんでいて、回復は難しいかもしれない。

百字要約　「段落要旨」を参考にして、本文全体の内容を百字程度の日本語で要約しなさい。

（下書き）

本文解説

1 【文構造】

(l.1) (S)Growing evidence / **that** countries **where** there is more inequality of income are places **where** there is less equality of opportunity // (V)**helps us understand** why the United States has become one of the advanced countries with the least equality of opportunity.

- ▶ that は同格節を導く接続詞。that 節中は countries are places が基本構造で、countries, places それぞれを where で始まる関係副詞節が修飾している。
- ▶ 〈help + O + (to) *do*〉で「O が〜するのを助ける」。why で始まる節は understand の目的語で、helps us understand why 〜 で「我々がなぜ〜かを理解するのを助けている」。
- ▶ Growing evidence helps us understand は、原因や理由となるものが「人に〜させる」という形の「無生物主語構文」なので、「〜という証拠がどんどん積み重なり、そのため私たちは、なぜ〜なのかを理解しやすくなっている」などと訳すとわかりやすい。

2 【補語を文頭に出した倒置文】【「…のうちで」の意味を表す of …】

(l.7) (C)Even more disastrous (V)is (S)how education perpetuates advantages and disadvantages: **of** Americans born around 1980, only about 9 percent **of** those from the bottom quarter of the income distribution graduated from college.

- ▶ 文の補語 (C) が文頭に置かれたために、主語 (S) と述語動詞 (V) が倒置されている。直前の文の内容を受けて、even more disastrous「それよりもさらに悲惨なのは〜だ」で始めて強調している。
- ▶ of Americans … と of those … の of は、「…のうちで」の意味。

3 【前置詞＋関係代名詞】

(l.27) Basic values **for which** the country has stood ― equality of opportunity, equal access to justice, a sense of a system that is fair ― have been eroded.

- ▶ for which the country has stood は、主語の Basic values を修飾している関係代名詞節。stand for … で「…を支持する」を意味し、関係代名詞 which が前置詞 for の目的語になっている。
- ▶ the country has stood for basic values「国（＝アメリカ合衆国）は基本的価値観を支持してきた」を基に、「国が支持してきた基本的価値観」は以下の 3 通りに表現できる。
  1) 前置詞を後ろに残し、関係代名詞を節の先頭に置く
     basic values which [あるいは that] the country has stood for
  2) 1) の関係代名詞を省略する
     basic values the country has stood for
  3) 前置詞を関係代名詞の直前に置く。この場合 for that は不可。
     basic values for which the country has stood
- ▶ ダッシュ（―）にはさまれた部分には、Basic values for which the country has stood の具体例が挙げられている。a sense of a system that is fair は a sense that a system is fair「制度が公正であるという感覚」の意味で、ここでは a general feeling that the country's system is fair ということ。
- ▶ この文全体の意味するところを言い換えると、以下のようになるだろう。
  The basic values that America has long promoted to the world, such as equality of opportunity, equal access to justice, and a sense of a system that is fair, have been weakened.

4 【simply … not】

(l.36) Although economists typically don't use words like "trust," in fact, our economy **simply can't** function without trust.

- ▶ 否定語の前に simply を置いた simply … not は否定の強調で、「全く…でない」の意味。just … not も同意。
  ex. I simply can't believe what has happened.「私は起こったことがとても信じられない」
- ▶ 否定語の後に simply を置いた not simply … は「単に…ではない」の意味。
  ex. Success is not simply a matter of luck.「成功とは単に運の問題ではない」

Memo

The first commercially available digital camera was launched in 1990. In the decade ✪66 that followed, it created a lot of anxiety in photographers and photography scholars. Some went as far as declaring photography dead as a result of this shift. Initially this was considered too steep a change to be classified as a reconfiguration⋆, rather (1)it was seen
5 as a break. A death of something old. A birth of something new.

Digital images can also be easily copied, duplicated and edited. The latter made the ✪67 flexibility of what photos can be seen as representing more obvious. It also made representing ourselves and our lives easy, cheap and quick. Additional shots now come with no additional costs, and we can and do take 10, 20, 30 snaps of any given thing to
10 sort through later. In addition to transforming the individual value of the image, (2)this has altered the emotional meanings we attributed both to keeping and getting rid of individual photographs. Printed images of loved ones used to be kept even if they were out of focus, blurry or had development mistakes on them. In the context of the massive amount of digital images, the labour of love now becomes the cleaning, sorting, tagging,
15 categorizing and deleting majority of the photos. While it is occasionally claimed that this emergent acceptance of deleting photos is indicative of their diminished social worth, there are plenty of digital snapshots that are printed out, displayed as the lock-screen on devices, or used as the background of the computer screen. Overall, we can say that digitalization has shifted the focus of photography from photographs themselves to the
20 act of taking pictures.

The first camera phones date back to the very beginning of the twenty-first century. ✪68 In early 2001, the BBC reported on the first cell phone with a camera invented in Japan. Readers from around the world offered their ideas on what such a peculiar invention might be good for. Some said it could have many uses for teenagers (streamlining
25 shopping for outfits, proving you have met a pop idol, setting up your friends on dates) but would be pretty pointless for adults. Others thought it would be a practical aid for spying, taking sneak pictures of your competitors' produce or quickly reporting traffic accidents and injuries. (3)Yet others thought it might be nice for travelers to keep in touch with their families or hobbyists to show art or collections to others. My personal
30 favourites include commenters who wrote they couldn't wait for the device to be available at a reasonable price in their home country, so they can take pictures of the

friendly dogs they meet at the park. Someone suggested the camera needs to be on the front to allow for video calls, which didn't happen in practice until 2003.

69   A digital culture scholar claims that the fact that we always carry a camera alters what can be and is seen, recorded, discussed and remembered. Some photography scholars   35 propose that camera phones and camera phone images have three social uses — to capture memories, to maintain relationships, and to express yourself. (4)In contrast, another scholar argues that the camera phone is no different from other portable image making devices and that the uses and meanings attributed to home videos in the 1980s have been exactly the same — memory, communication and self-expression. In this   40 sense, the social function of photography seems to have remained despite the changes through various reconfigurations of technology and cultural imaginaries about it.

   *   reconfiguration = modification; redesign

解答欄

1
....

2
....
....
....
....

3
....
....
....
....
....

4
....
....
....
....

語句　音声は、「英語」→「日本語の意味」の順で読まれます。　　　CD 2- Tr 70-73

入試基礎レベル

8　**shot** [ʃát]（名）

10　**image** [ímidʒ]（名）

11　**emotional** [imóuʃənəl]

17　**display** [displéi]（動）

26　**aid** [éid]（名）

41　**function** [fʌ́nkʃən]（名）

入試標準レベル（共通テスト・私大）

1　**launch** [lɔ́:ntʃ]（動）

2　**anxiety** [æŋzáiəti]

2　**photography** [fətágrəfi]

2　**scholar** [skálər]

3　**declare A (to be) B**

3　**shift** [ʃíft]（名）

3　**initially** [iníʃəli]

4　**classify A as B**

6　**edit** [édit]（動）

7　**represent** [rèprizént]

10　**transform** [trænsfɔ́:rm]（動）

11　**alter** [ɔ́:ltər]

11　**attribute A to B**

13　**in the context of ...**

13　**massive** [mǽsiv]

16　**emergent** [imɔ́:rdʒənt]（形）

16　**acceptance** [əkséptəns]

18　**device** [diváis]

19　**shift** [ʃíft]（動）

23　**peculiar** [pikjú:ljər]

26　**practical** [prǽktikəl]

33　**allow for ...**

33　**in practice**

37　**capture** [kǽptʃər]（動）

38　**be no different from ...**

38　**portable** [pɔ́:rtəbl]（形）

入試発展レベル（二次・有名私大）

1　**commercially available**

4　**steep** [stí:p]（形）

7　**flexibility** [flèksəbíləti]

9　**any given ...**

13　**out of focus**

15　**categorize** [kǽtigəràiz]

15　**delete** [dilí:t]（動）

16　**diminished** [dimíniʃt]（形）

27　**competitor** [kəmpétətər]

40　**self-expression**

その他

3　**go as far as** *doing*　〜しさえする

4　**reconfiguration** [rìkənfigjəréiʃən]
　再設計、再構成

5　**break** [bréik]（名）　断絶、絶縁

6　**duplicate** [djú:plikèit]（動）
　複製する

6　**the latter**　後者、最後のもの

10　**sort through ...**　…を仕分けて整理する

13　**blurry** [blɔ́:ri]　ぼやけた

13　**development** [divéləpmənt]
　（写真の）現像

14　**labour of love**　好きでする仕事

14　**tag** [tǽg]（動）　タグ [札] をつける

16　**be indicative of ...**　…を示して [暗示して]

17　**snapshot** [snǽpʃàt]（名）　スナップ写真

17　**lock-screen**　ロック画面

19　**digitalization** [dìdʒətəlaizéiʃən]
　デジタル化

24　**streamline** [strí:mlàin]（動）
　効率化する、簡素化する

25　**outfit** [áutfìt]（名）　衣服、服装

25　**pop idol**　アイドル歌手

25　**set up ... on a date**　…のデートをお膳立てする

26　**pointless** [pɔ́intlis]　無意味な、無益な

27　**spy** [spái]（動）　スパイ活動をする

27　**sneak** [sní:k]（形）　内密の、盗み見的な

29　**hobbyist** [hábist]　趣味に熱中する人

42　**cultural imaginary**　文化的に想像されるもの

展開	段落	要旨
主題の 提示	1	1990年の（①　　　　　　　　　）の出現は写真の世界に急激な変化と不安をもたらし、再構成 ではなく断絶とすら見なされた。
主題の 展開①	2	大量撮影や編集を可能とした写真のデジタル化は、画像の個々の価値だけでなく、写真管理に私 たちが込めていた（②　　　　　　）意味合いを変えた。写真撮影の焦点は、写真そのものから（③ 　　　　　）へと移行した。
主題の 展開②	3	最初の（④　　　　　　　　　）が発明されると、その価値や実用性、用途などをめぐって様々 な反応や提案があった。
主題の 展開③	4	（④　　　　　　　　　　　　）とその画像の社会的用途は、記録、コミュニケーション、 （⑤　　　　　　　）だとする主張がある。そして、それらは1980年代の（⑥　　　　　　　）の 用途や意味と全く同じだと言う人もいる。その点では、写真撮影の社会的機能は変わらないまま だと言える。

百字要約　「段落要旨」を参考にして、本文全体の内容を百字程度の日本語で要約しなさい。

（下書き）

<!-- 原稿用紙（空欄） -->

本文解説

1 【classify A as B, see A as B】【rather の用法】

(l.3)　Initially this was considered too steep a change to **be classified as** a reconfiguration, **rather** it **was seen** as a break.

▶ この文は "Initially this was considered too steep a change to be classified as a reconfiguration; rather, it was seen as a break." と、rather の前にセミコロン (;) を置いた方が意味が明確になるだろう。

▶ this は前文（第 1 段落第 3 文）の this shift「この変化＝デジタルカメラの出現が生み出した変化」を指す。too steep a change to be classified は too ... to *do* 構文で、「（～と）分類するにはあまりにも急激な変化」の意味。「急激な変化」は a steep change だが、too が加わると〈too ＋形容詞＋ a［an］＋名詞〉の語順になることに注意。

▶ rather「むしろ、そうではなく（＝ instead）、それどころか」が 2 文をつなぐ接続詞的な働きをしている。it was seen ... の it も this（＝ this shift）を受け、rather, it was seen as a break で「むしろ、それ（＝その変化）は断絶だと見なされた」。

▶ classify A as B「A を B と分類する」と、see A as B「A を B と見なす」はどちらも受動態になっている。

2 【文構造】

(l.6)　(S)The latter (V)made (O)the flexibility of what photos can be seen as representing (C)more obvious.

(l.7)　(S)It also (V)made (O)representing ourselves and our lives (C)easy, cheap and quick.

▶ 2 文とも SVOC の文型。それぞれ「S が O をより明らかにした」、「S が O を容易に、安価に、迅速にした」という意味。

【第 1 文】

▶ the latter は 2 つの場合は「後者」を、3 つ以上の場合には「最後のもの」を指す。ここでは、前文の Digital images can also be easily copied, duplicated and edited. の 3 つ目、"(can be) edited" を指す。無生物主語なので、「最後の（編集の）機能によって～がより明らかになった」などと訳すと自然。

▶ can be seen as ... は can see A as ...「A を…と見なす［考える］ことができる」の受動態。
photos can be seen as representing ～「写真は～を表現していると考えうる」
→ what photos can be seen as representing「写真が表現していると考えうるもの」
→ the flexibility of what photos can be seen as representing「写真が表現していると考えられるものの柔軟性」

▶ 全体を、"The latter made it more obvious that what photos can be seen as representing is flexible." と表現することもできる。

【第 2 文】

▶ It は前文の The latter を受けている。representing ourselves and our lives は動名詞句で、「私たち自身や私たちの生活を表現すること」。

3 【文構造】【be indicative of ...】

(l.15)　While it is occasionally claimed that this emergent acceptance of deleting photos **is indicative of** their diminished social worth, there are plenty of digital snapshots that are printed out, displayed as the lock-screen on devices, or used as the background of the computer screen.

▶ While が導く従属節は it is occasionally ... social worth で、there are 以下が主節となる。

▶ 接続詞 while はここでは〈譲歩〉〈対照〉を表し、「～ではあるが（although）、～の一方で（whereas）」。it is occasionally claimed that の it は形式主語で、真主語は that 以下 social worth までの名詞節。

- ▶ emergent は動詞 emerge の形容詞形で、「新しく出現した」の意味。acceptance of deleting photos は、accept deleting photos「写真の削除を受け入れる」の名詞表現と考えるとよい。this emergent acceptance of deleting photos は、this growing acceptance of deleting photos あるいは the increased acceptance of deleting photos の意味で、「このように写真の削除を受け入れるようになってきていること」。

- ▶ indicative は動詞 indicate の形容詞形。be indicative of ... で「…を示して[暗示して]いる」。their diminished social worth の their は photos を受けている。

- ▶ that are printed の that は plenty of digital snapshots を先行詞とする関係代名詞で、are printed, (are) displayed, (are) used の3つの受動態が続いている。

- ▶ as the lock-screen on devices と as the background of the computer screen の as ... は、「…として」の意味。

❹ 【wait for A to *do*】【so (that) S+V 〜】

(l.29) My personal favourites include commenters who wrote they couldn't **wait for** the device **to be** available at a reasonable price in their home country, **so** they can take pictures of the friendly dogs they meet at the park.

- ▶ who 以下は commenters を先行詞とする関係代名詞節。wrote の後に接続詞 that が省略されている。wait for the device to be available ... は wait for A to *do*「Aが〜するのを待つ」の構造。couldn't wait は「(〜が)待ちきれない、待ち遠しい」という気持ちを表している。

- ▶ so they can take ... は、〈目的〉あるいは〈結果〉を表す〈so that S+V 〜〉の that が省かれたもので、for the device to be available at a reasonable price in their home country「この機器が自分の国で手ごろな値段で手に入る」を修飾する副詞節と考えられる。この構文では、so の直前にコンマがあるときは〈結果〉の意味を表すことが多いが、絶対ではない。ここも、「彼らが…の写真を撮れるように」〈目的〉、「そうすれば…の写真を撮れるようになる」〈結果〉のどちらにも解釈できる。

- ▶ commenter は「コメントを寄せる個人、ブログなどにコメントを投稿する人」のこと。commentator「解説者、評論家、(テレビ・ラジオなどの)実況解説者、実況アナウンサー」とは違う。

【native speaker の見解】
In this sentence, "..., so they <u>can</u> take pictures ..." should be "..., so they <u>could</u> take pictures ...".

❺ 【文構造】【受動態の意味】

(l.34) A digital culture scholar claims that the fact that we always carry a camera alters what **can be** and **is seen, recorded, discussed and remembered**.

- ▶ that the fact ... remembered が動詞 claims の目的語となる名詞節。その節の構造は、_(S)<u>the fact that we always carry a camera</u> _(V)<u>alters</u> _(O)<u>what can be ... remembered</u>

- ▶ the fact that 〜の that は同格節を導く接続詞で、「〜という事実」。

- ▶ what can be and is seen, recorded, discussed and remembered は、can be と is のそれぞれに seen, recorded, discussed and remembered の4つの過去分詞がつながって受動態を作っている。〈can be ＋過去分詞〉は「〜される可能性がある」、〈is ＋過去分詞〉は「実際に〜されている」の意味。全体で「見られ、記録され、議論され、記憶される可能性があるし、また実際にそうされているもの」。

Rumours spread by two different but overlapping processes: popular confirmation ⊘74 and in-group momentum. The first occurs because each of us tends to rely on what others think and do. Once a certain number of people appear to believe a rumour, others will believe it too, unless they have good reason to think it is false. Most rumours

5 involve topics on which people lack direct or personal knowledge, and so most of us often simply trust the crowd. As more people accept the crowd view, the crowd grows larger, creating a real risk that large groups of people will believe rumours even though they are completely false.

In-group momentum refers to the fact that when like-minded people get together, ⊘75

10 they often end up believing a more extreme version of what they thought before. Suppose that members of a certain group are inclined to accept a rumour about, say, the evil intentions of a certain nation. In all likelihood, they will become more committed to that rumour after they have spoken to each other. (1)Indeed, they may move from being tentative believers to being absolutely certain, even though their only new evidence

15 is what other members of the group believe. Consider the role of the internet here: when people see many tweets or posts from like-minded people, they are strongly inclined to accept a rumour as true.

(2)What can be done to reduce the risk that these two processes will lead us to ⊘76 accept false rumours? The most obvious answer, and the standard one, involves the

20 system of free expression: people should be exposed to balanced information and to corrections from those who know the truth. Freedom usually works, but in some contexts (3)it is an incomplete remedy. People do not process information in a neutral way, and emotions often get in the way of truth. People take in new information in a very uneven way, and those who have accepted false rumours do not easily give up

25 their beliefs, especially when there are strong emotional commitments involved. It can be extremely hard to change what people think, even by presenting them with facts.

1 popular confirmation

10 20

in-group momentum

10 20

2

3

4

5

10 20

（下書き） 10 20

語句　音声は、「英語」→「日本語の意味」の順で読まれます。　　　CD 2 - Tr 77-80

入試基礎レベル

1　**rumour** [rú:mər]（名）　......................

1　**spread** [spréd]（動）　......................

3　**once ~**（接）　......................

3　**appear to** *do*　......................

6　**crowd** [kráud]（名）　......................

12　**evil** [í:v(ə)l]（形）　......................

23　**take in ...**　......................

入試標準レベル（共通テスト・私大）

1　**process** [prásəs]（名）　......................

3　**a certain number of ...**
....

4　**good reason**　十分［もっとも］な理由

4　**false** [fɔ́:ls]　......................

5　**personal** [pə́:rsənəl]　......................

6　**view** [vjú:]（名）　......................

10　**extreme** [ikstrí:m]　......................

11　**be inclined to** *do*　......................

11　**say** [séi]（副）　......................

12　**intention** [inténʃən]　......................

12　**(be) committed to ...**　......................

14　**absolutely** [ǽbsəlù:tli]　......................

16　**post** [póust]（名）　投稿......................

20　**be exposed to ...**　......................

21　**work** [wə́:rk]（動）　うまく機能する

22　**context** [kántekst]　......................

22　**process** [prásəs]（動）　......................

22　**neutral** [njú:trəl]（形）　......................

25　**emotional** [imóuʃənəl]　......................

25　**commitment** [kəmítmənt]
....

26　**present A with B**

入試発展レベル（二次・有名私大）

1　**overlap** [òuvərlǽp]（動）　......................

1　**confirmation** [kànfərméiʃən]
....

10　**version** [və́:rʒən]　説明、見解、意見

12　**in all likelihood**

18　**lead A to** *do*

20　**balanced** [bǽlənst]（形）

21　**correction** [kərékʃən]

22　**incomplete** [inkəmplí:t]（形）
....

22　**remedy** [rémədi]（名）　......................

23　**get in the way of ...**　......................

24　**uneven** [ʌní:vən]　......................

その他

2　**in-group**　内集団、(排他的) 仲間集団

2　**momentum** [mouméntəm]
勢い、はずみ

9　**like-minded**（形）　同じ考えを持った

14　**tentative** [téntətiv]（形）　一時的な、ためらいがちな

16　**tweet** [twí:t]（名）　ツイート、つぶやき

段落要旨　各段落のまとめとなるように、空所に適切な語句を入れなさい。（同じ番号には、同じ語句が入ります）

展開	段落	要旨
主題の提示①	1	うわさの広まり方には２つの（①　　　　　）がある。１つは、あるうわさを大勢の人々が信じていると、他の人もそれを単純に信用してしまうという「（②　　　　　　）」。
主題の提示②	2	もう１つは、同じ考え方を持つ人々から成る集団内で、考えがより（③　　　　　）になっていくという「（④　　　　　）」。
主題の展開	3	誤ったうわさを防ぐには、公平かつ公正な情報に触れることが必要だ。しかし、人々は情報を偏って処理し、しばしば（⑤　　　　　　）に邪魔されることがあるため、人々の考えを変えることは極めて困難な場合がある。

百字要約　「段落要旨」を参考にして、本文全体の内容を百字程度の日本語で要約しなさい。

（下書き）

10　　　　　　　　　　　　　　　　20

10　　　　　　　　　　　　　　　　20

本文解説

1 【as の用法】【分詞構文】【同格節を導く that】

(l.6) **As more people** accept the crowd view, the crowd grows **larger, creating a real risk that** large groups of people will believe rumours even though they are completely false.

(l.18) What can be done to reduce **the risk that** these two processes will lead us to accept false rumours?

【第1文】 ▶ As more people ... の接続詞 as は「〜するにつれて、〜するに従って」の意味を表し、この文のように比較級を伴うことが多い。
　　▶ creating 以下の分詞構文は、主節の「その集団はさらに大きくなる」結果として起きることを述べている。and it creates a real risk that ... あるいは , which creates a real risk that ... と書き換えられる。
　　▶ that large groups of people ... の that は、直前の a real risk に対して〈同格〉の名詞節を導く接続詞で、「〜という現実的な危険」。
【第2文】 the risk that ... の that も、上記の that と同じく〈同格〉の名詞節を導く接続詞。lead A to do は「(誤った考えなどを抱かせて) A に〜させる」。

2 【refer to ...】【同格節を導く that】【end up *doing*】

(l.9) In-group momentum **refers to the fact that** when like-minded people get together, they often **end up believing** a more extreme version of what they thought before.

　　▶ refer to ... で「(言葉・数字などが) …を指す [示す、表す]」。
　　▶ that は the fact と〈同格〉の名詞節を導く接続詞。ここでは、その名詞節が〈when S´+V´ 〜, S+V 〜〉という複文になっている。
　　▶ end up *doing*「(最後には) 〜することになる」
　　▶ a more extreme version of what they thought before は「以前の考えがより極端になったもの」という意味。version は、ここでは「(物事に対する) 見解、解釈、説明 (= an account or description from a particular point of view especially as contrasted with another account)」の意味。

3 【in all likelihood】【(be) committed to ...】

(l.12) **In all likelihood**, they will become more **committed to** that rumour after they have spoken to each other.

　　▶ in all likelihood「おそらく、ほとんど確実に、十中八九 (= almost certainly)」
　　▶ (be) committed to ... で「…に熱心である、…に傾倒している、…に真剣に取り組む (= willing to work very hard at something)」。they will become more committed to that rumour after 〜で「〜の後の方が、そのうわさをより強く信じるようになるだろう」といった意味。

4 【get in the way of ...】

(l.22) People do not process information in a neutral way, and emotions often **get in the way of** truth.

　　▶ get in the way of ... で「…の邪魔をする、…を妨げる (= to prevent someone from doing something, or prevent something from happening)」。
　　ex. I don't want anyone to get in the way of my current lifestyle.
　　　　「私は今の生活を誰にも邪魔されたくない」

5 【It can be ... to *do*】【by *doing*】【present A with B】

(l.25) **It can be** extremely hard **to change** what people think, even **by presenting them with facts**.

　　▶ It は形式主語で、真主語は to change 以下。It can be 〜「〜ということがありうる、〜のこともある」。
　　▶ even by *doing* で「〜することによっても、たとえ〜しても」。〈by +動名詞〉で「手段」を表している。
　　▶ present A with B「A に B を提示する」

2024.1

Cutting Edge Orange
Navi Book

カッティングエッジ・オレンジ
ナビブック 〔付録〕

検印欄

1	2	3	4	5	6
7	8	9	10	11	12
13	14	15	16		

年　　　　組　　　　番　氏名